WILLIAM "BIL.

KNOCK OUT
YOUR RETIREMENT
INCOME WORRIES
FOREVER

THE ULTIMATE TRAINING GUIDE
FOR DEVELOPING FINANCIAL SECURITY

WILLIAM "BILL" SMITH

KNOCK OUT
YOUR RETIREMENT
INCOME WORRIES
FOREVER

THE ULTIMATE TRAINING GUIDE
FOR DEVELOPING FINANCIAL SECURITY

Published by Advantage, Charleston, South Carolina.
Member of Advantage Media Group.

ADVANTAGE is a registered trademark and the Advantage colophon is a trademark of Advantage Media Group, Inc.

Printed in the United States of America.

ISBN: 978-159932-311-4
LCCN: 2011942504

This publication is designed to provide accurate and authoritative information in regard to the subject matter covered. It is sold with the understanding that the publisher is not engaged in rendering legal, accounting, or other professional services. If legal advice or other expert assistance is required, the services of a competent professional person should be sought.

Advantage Media Group is proud to be a part of the Tree Neutral® program. Tree Neutral offsets the number of trees consumed in the production and printing of this book by taking proactive steps such as planting trees in direct proportion to the number of trees used to print books. To learn more about Tree Neutral, please visit **www.treeneutral.com**. To learn more about Advantage's commitment to being a responsible steward of the environment, please visit **www.advantagefamily.com/green**

William A. Smith is a licensed insurance representative in the state of Ohio. His license number is 21538. Investment Advisory Services are offered through Great Lakes Retirement, Inc., an Ohio Registered Investment Advisor. His National Producer Number is 2441157.

ABOUT THE AUTHOR

 **William "Bill" Smith, RFC,** is a nationally recognized financial advisor who specializes in retirement income planning and the protection of assets. He is the president and CEO of W.A. Smith Financial Group, an Ohio-based retirement planning firm. He is also the chief advisor for Great Lakes Retirement, Inc., a registered investment advisor in the state of Ohio. His firms manage in excess of $100 million.

Since 1995 Bill has educated thousands of people in his retirement classes. Throughout all of his endeavors, his main goal is to empower retirees and pre-retirees to make smarter decisions with their money.

Bill is often sought out by local and national news affiliates because of his expertise. He has appeared in the *Wall Street Journal, Smart Money* magazine, *Senior Market Advisor* magazine, theStreet.com, AOL's Daily Finance, SecondAct.com, as well as many others. He often appears on local TV news channels as well as in newspapers throughout his area.

Each week Bill extends his knowledge and education to thousands of listeners as the host of the popular radio show, *Retirement Matters.*

Bill is a Registered Financial Consultant, an Investment Advisor Representative, and a licensed insurance professional in the state of Ohio. He graduated from the University of Akron.

CONTENTS

REGULATORY ISSUES

The following authored publication contains the ideas of its author. Any strategies, ideas, notes, or recommendations that are outlined in this book may not be suitable for everyone. They are not guaranteed or warranted to produce any particular or specific results. The presentation or listing of specific data that was used in conjunction with any example does not imply that similar results will be obtained either now, or at any point in the future. This data is merely provided for an illustrative purpose and for the sake of discussion. Readers should focus on the principles that these illustrations or examples support rather than the periods or results listed.

This book is distributed and/or sold with the understanding that neither the publisher nor the author, through this book, is engaged in rendering legal, tax, investment, insurance, financial, accounting, or any other professional advice or services. If the reader requires said advice, he/she should consult with the recommended professional for said services.

We make no warranty with respect to the accuracy or the completeness of the information contained in this publication. The author and the publisher, together, disclaim any responsibility or liability associated with the loss or injury, personal or otherwise, that is incurred as a direct or indirect result of following principles or strategies outlined in this publication.

Finally, this book is written under the authority of the first amendment to the Constitution of the United States of America.

THE END

Successful people in retirement never lose sight of the end – the retirement situation, or goal, they have set for themselves. Unfortunately, over the past two decades, I have personally witnessed all too many results of poor retirement planning.

People dying and giving away 80% of their estates to greedy politicians (our government) and bloodthirsty attorneys... Individuals losing their life savings due to a devastating long-term illness... And, perhaps worst of all, people whose life savings have been crushed on Wall Street, forcing them into poverty or returning to work because they need the income to survive.

To quote Stephen Covey, "Begin with the end in mind." The folks above failed to plan with their respective ends in mind. But here's the thing: One way or another, the end is inevitable.

There are a lot of people who die climbing Mount Everest. The most amazing thing about this is that the majority die on the way down the mountain, not on the way up. Is it possible that the people who died forgot that the end was not the summit of Mount Everest, rather it was more about making it back down the mountain alive?

Retirement is really no different. Just because you make it *to* retirement doesn't mean that you will make it *through* retirement – unless you never lose sight of your goals, you never lose sight of "the end."

What do you want your end to be?

In my experience interviewing and speaking to thousands of people, for most it's about:

- Having guaranteed income that will support their lifestyle as long as they live
- Safety of their money
- Paying the least amount of taxes
- Protection of their assets
- Distribution of their remaining assets to their heirs in the most tax-advantageous way possible

So, with the end in mind, I share with you these keys to making it to, and through, retirement:

- **Don't go it alone**
- **Hire the right advisor**
- **Educate yourself**
- **Trust your feelings**

This book is dedicated to the people who want to protect their life savings and keep more of what they have accumulated during their lifetime. I want to empower you to make smarter choices with your money. In the end you will have guaranteed income that no one can take away from you.

My goal for you, the reader, is that after reading this book, you will never lose sight of the end.

CHAPTER 1

RETIRED WITH TWO BROKEN LEGS

Don't rely on the bankrupt government or greedy corporations for your retirement. The responsibility is YOURS.

Have you ever heard the "three-legged stool" metaphor about retirement income? In the old days it was used to illustrate the three most common sources of retirement income: Social Security, employee pensions and personal savings. Like the legs of a stool, these three sources of income, together, were counted 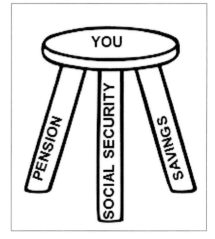 on for steady, reliable support during people's later years. And it worked, to a point. But that was a different time, and the world was a much different place.

In this book we'll talk a little about then, more about now, and even more about planning for tomorrow. For now, though, just take my word for it: Forget the stool.

It's rickety at best, and when you really start inspecting it you can see how weak and unstable at least two of its legs are. Maybe you can salvage a few pieces here and there, but basically, it's time to build a new stool. But first let's take a look at what went wrong with the old one.

LEG ONE: SOCIAL SECURITY

Social Security is currently the largest social welfare program in the United States, constituting 37% of government expenditure and 7% of GDP. It was created in 1935 as part of the New Deal. At that time the average life expectancy was 62 years old – 16 years less than it is today.

The plan was never intended to provide retirement income to nearly 60 million people, as it does today, much less to the more than 70 million baby boomers expected to be over age 65 by 2030.

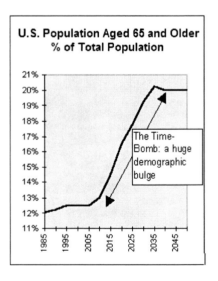

U.S. Population Aged 65 and Older % of Total Population

The Time-Bomb: a huge demographic bulge

Between 2011 and 2030 it is projected that approximately 10,000 people will turn 65 every day for the next 19 years, increasing the number of people eligible for Social Security benefits by 62%, while the number of people paying Social Security taxes will increase by only 17%. You do the math.

It says right on the front of the Social Security statement you receive each year that Social Security will go into a

---

Did you know...

When FDR introduced the Social Security program, he promised that the money put into the independent trust fund would never be used to fund any other government program – or be taxed![1]

---

negative cash flow in 2016 and will be bankrupt in 2037, only able to pay 76 cents out of every dollar that's promised on your Social Security statement at that time.

Surprise! Because of high unemployment and the recent turmoil in our economy, Social Security has *already* gone into negative cash flow.[2] Going forward, you'll still get your payments, but what will they be worth with no cost-of-living rider built into the program? What will they be worth if you have to pay higher taxes to keep the benefit? What will they be worth if you're not eligible to receive your full benefits until you're 70, 72 or perhaps even 75 years old?

Questions like these may not be pleasant to ponder, but it's important that you do. Perhaps the most important question to ask yourself is, do you feel safe relying on Social

Security as a primary source – or *the* primary source – of your retirement income? I certainly wouldn't.

LEG TWO: DEFINED PENSIONS AND 401(K) PLANS

Let's turn back the clock again, this time to review the good old-fashioned defined benefit pension plan. Prior to the 1980s, when many employers began shifting to 401(k) programs, the pension was an all-but-guaranteed source of steady income after retirement.

The amount of pension benefits received depended on how long a person worked at a company (or institution or government entity) and at what age they stopped working there. From these figures employers calculated precisely how much the person would receive in monthly or annual pension benefits after retirement.

Simple, predictable, defined – that is, unless a company goes bust or its pension is otherwise underfunded. Although most employers have phased out defined benefit pensions, they are still responsible for paying out the benefits owed to the now mostly retired employees who worked there when the pension plan was in place.

It is estimated that the average pension fund today is funded at only 78% of the benefits promised. Where does the other 22% come from? Good question. In some cases taxes have – or will be – increased to cover state and other publicly funded pensions that can't otherwise pay out the promised benefits. In the private sector, any benefits earned under a defined benefit plan to date are protected by the PBGC (Pension Benefit Guarantee Corporation) – to a certain extent, anyway. In 2010, non-union Delphi workers lost anywhere from 30% to 70% of their pension benefits when the PBGC

Did you know...

In the United States, unfunded pension liabilities equal up to $3.2 trillion![3]

took over benefit payments for the bankrupt company. Either way, employers have begun to do away with these expensive plans as they flee to 401(k)s.

OK, let's talk about 401(k) plans, which have virtually replaced defined pension programs in the private sector. They can vary from company to company, but the general idea is that employees designate a certain percentage (or dollar amount) from their earnings to be automatically deposited in their 401(k) accounts. Usually they have several categories to choose from (all of which have fancy names that are probably unfamiliar to you). You select where you want your money to be invested – for example, 25% in company stock, 50% in mutual funds, and so on.

So you've got a kind of forced savings plan, which is good; but you have to make investment decisions about it, which for most people isn't so good without professional guidance. At least it's some form of savings, though, and it's relatively low risk – or so people thought!

Then all economic hell broke loose. The ever-climbing 401(k) numbers people were used to seeing on their statements took an abrupt downward turn, bursting many a nest-egg bubble. The proceeds from their various invest-

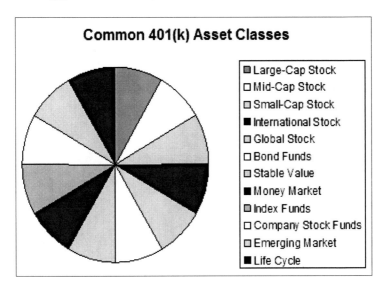

Common 401(k) Asset Classes

- ▨ Large-Cap Stock
- ▢ Mid-Cap Stock
- ▢ Small-Cap Stock
- ■ International Stock
- ▢ Global Stock
- ▢ Bond Funds
- ▨ Stable Value
- ■ Money Market
- ▨ Index Funds
- ▢ Company Stock Funds
- ▨ Emerging Market
- ■ Life Cycle

ments tumbled – not at all like the steadily growing totals they had been seeing on their statements in previous years. The downturn caused approximately 27% of workers age 45 and above to delay their retirement.

And for many people it got worse from there.

Say you had $250,000 socked away in your 401(k) for retirement, and you were laid off. The economy bottoms out and you can't find another job. You go through what little savings you have, and now you're faced with either losing your home or dipping into your 401(k) account, even though there are huge penalties and taxes for early withdrawals.

The responsibility is yours, so you will always have the temptation to spend the money you have accumulated. What do you do? Raid the 401(k) and start kissing your retirement savings goodbye?

Unfortunately, there is a common denominator for the 27% of people who will delay retirement and the millions of people across the country that lost chunks of their retirement nest egg: no protected money. Because most investors had all of their money at risk, they were not protected from loss when the markets fell in 2008 and 2009.

And that brings us to the third leg of the stool.

LEG THREE: PERSONAL SAVINGS

We all know we should, but most people don't. Exercise? Eat right? Floss their teeth? Perhaps, but that's not what I'm talking about.

I'm talking about saving money for retirement. With the other two legs of the stool barely standing, it's more important than ever to shore up that third leg. Meanwhile, what are most people doing?

1. Trying to make ends meet today and avoiding thinking about tomorrow.

2. Assuming that between Social Security and pension benefits they'll have enough income to maintain their standard of living after they've retired.

3. Setting some money aside, but not really knowing how to leverage it into reliable, accessible income during retirement.

4. Basing the amount of retirement income they'll need on current numbers, without taking inflation, increased taxes, higher healthcare costs and longer life expectancy into consideration.

5. All of the above.

WHERE DOES THIS LEAVE US?

Here's the reality: Of working households across the U.S. today, 51% are at risk of not being able to maintain their standard of living after they've retired.

A lot of people simply can't retire. Others retire, discover they can't pay their bills, and then have to go back to work – that is, if they can find work. Still others simply don't know what to do.

If any of these describe you, you're not alone. A solution is not beyond your grasp. You just have to separate yourself from all the "could have, should have" thinking and focus on creating a secure retirement income for yourself – a brand new stool custom-made for you to "sit" on and know you'll be OK in retirement.

Yes, you can do this. And yes, you'll need some guidance along the way.

So let's get started.

CHAPTER 2

WHY MOST RETIRED INVESTORS FAIL

Even the smartest people can – and often do – make terrible investment decisions. Your challenge is to defend yourself from your own desires, thoughts and emotions that can seriously flaw your investment choices.

W hat I'm going to say in this chapter might be tough to take, but believe me, you need to hear it. It will help save *you* from *yourself* as you make important decisions about your future security.

Why are many people their own worst enemies when it comes to money choices? Believe it or not, there's an entire field of study devoted to answering that question. Known as behavioral economics, the science combines psychology and economic theory to examine social, cognitive and emotional factors affecting financial decisions as well as the broad outcomes of these decisions. It's a fascinating field, well-deserving of a closer look by consumers, borrowers, investors, businesses and governments alike.

For our purposes, though, we'll focus on key findings directly relating to individual investors and remedies for common behaviors that get in the way of successful retirement planning.

LACK OF CLARITY

"I know I need a lot of money to retire, but I don't know exactly how much or how to get there."

The first step is figuring out how much retirement income you'll need to maintain a secure, comfortable lifestyle. **Notice I didn't say how much in retirement *assets*; I said how much retirement *income*.** It's a big difference, and understanding that from the beginning changes every step of the retirement planning process – in many cases ameliorating the obstacles explained below.

Let's expand on this idea with a hypothetical example. Let's say you're interviewing for a job and I said:

If you take this job, it comes with a retirement pension that will guarantee 5% to 8% annual growth for your retirement income. If you retire at age 60 you'll get to withdraw 5% of the balance in your retirement pension every year, no matter what, for the rest of your life. The amount of the first withdrawal you take, the withdrawal you take when your account is at its highest point, will remain the same each year for the rest of your life. Even if your account balance goes to zero, you'll still get the same check in the mail every single year until death. You can never run out of money as long as you live. Does that sound good?

What do you think you would say? Where do I sign!

Most people would let their behavior get in the way of their curiosity. You might tell me, "Well, that sounds too good to be true, Bill. You know what they say: 'If it sounds too good to be true, it probably is!'"

The crazy part about this scenario is that it's not so far-fetched. There are known strategies that can provide you with the type of retirement income I described. However, most average investors let their psyches get in the way of making the right decisions to make it happen.

Did you know...

"Investors diligently seek investments that they hope will produce the best returns, but they lose much of that benefit when they yield to psychological factors."[4]

> – Louis S. Harvey,
> president of DALBAR,
> a leading financial services
> market research firm

In Chapter 5 we'll go into detail about how to determine your retirement income needs (or "your number," as we call it in our office). For now, though, keep your eye toward establishing a concrete retirement income goal, and don't get beat up financially because of fuzzy vision – or none at all!

RATIONAL VS. EMOTIONAL DECISIONS

"If an investment of mine is gaining, I feel smart, like a winner. If it's losing, I look to blame my advisor."

This is just one of hundreds of examples of our natural tendency to view financial situations emotionally rather than rationally. I'm not implying we should be unfeeling zombies about everything having to do with money. I'm just saying that our decisions must be led by facts and reason.

Say, for example, you're holding on to a lousy investment because you think (or hope) it's going to rebound. Plus, maybe you don't want to admit to yourself or others that it was a dud in the first place.

Beyond a hunch or personal pride, however, there are dozens of other behaviors that play into money decisions – particularly the tendency to keep bad investments.

INVESTING DOESN'T HAVE TO BE A ROLLER COASTER RIDE!

If you're holding on to losers, be aware that it's just human nature to do so, but not necessarily the wisest investment choice.[5] In general, we don't like to admit we made a mistake. Why would we cut our losses when there's a possibility we could make back what we lost – thus redeeming our original less than brilliant decision? A lot of people are so focused on what they originally put into an investment and how much it's either up or down from that point, that they can't view it in a broader landscape that includes taxes, inflation, interest rates and personal considerations.

Here's an example of something I see a lot:

> *Mr. and Mrs. Jones make an initial investment of $500,000 into an asset allocation of stocks, bonds and mutual funds. Over the next two years the market rapidly declines and their original investment is now worth $250,000. They lost 50%.*
>
> *Rather than selling it then and there and moving to something where they can't lose more, they decide they'll wait until it gets back to $500,000 before they sell. Only now they don't need just 50% to get back to even; they need a 100% return.*
>
> *What are the odds that the stock market declines sharply again in the next five to 10 years while they wait for their account to achieve a 100% return so they can sell where they started?*

So, the stock went down. It could have gone up. Stop kicking yourself – or your advisor – and move on. Remember, your focus now is on safe and reliable retirement income, not risk and returns.

Let me say it again: **Your focus now is on safe and reliable retirement income, not risk and returns.**

INVESTING WITH THE HERD

"I know how to invest. I get lots of good advice from the guys at work, and I watch all the financial shows on TV. Everyone's going into mutual funds, gold and commodities right now. How can they all be wrong?"

From the Dutch tulip mania of the 1630s, to the dot-com bubble of the late 1990s, to today's fascination in gold and other hard commodities, a lot people just figure that if others are doing it, it must be the right thing to do. One herd watches FOX to get confirmation of their way of thinking; another watches MSNBC for theirs. Others turn to internet forums, golf buddies, the neighbor up the street, and the list goes on.

We have a natural bias toward information that says we're right. Conversely, we tend to discount information that says we're wrong. Don't blame yourself. Again, it's just human nature. If you're tempted to make an investment

---

We have a natural bias toward information that says we're right. Conversely, we tend to discount information that says we're wrong. Don't blame yourself.

---

choice just because someone – or a whole herd – is doing or recommending it, think again. Depend on empirical facts, not primal instincts.

FEAR AND GREED

"I've worked a lifetime to save my money, and it's not worth half what it used to be. I've got to get it back up to where it was before."

Stop right there. Once you retire you're not in the business of accumulating money or growing your assets anymore. You're in fixed income mode, meaning that your investment priority should be protecting your assets and making your savings last.

In Chapter 4 we're going to go over this in detail. Briefly, though, stop obsessing about "lost" money and getting it back. It's just a fact that the market moves in cycles. Economies have to be able to expand and contract; it has always been that way. (Bottom line: If you're not prepared to lose money, don't invest in something that can go down in value.)

Yes, many people entering retirement now are facing the reality of a downward cycle and its impact on the market-sensitive portion(s) of their retirement portfolios. This only underscores the importance of focusing on retirement income rather than assets.

Fear about losing money and the greed for more lead to extremely bad investment decisions – irreparable, even – and that's the last thing you need, especially now.

DECISION PARALYSIS

"This is important stuff that will directly affect my lifestyle, my future and my family's future. What if I make a mistake?"

Ever heard the saying, "Going from the frying pan into the fire?" It's a scientifically proven fact that the more choices people have, the more likely they are to put off making a decision. Who wants to jump in the fire? Given the tens of thousands of ways to spend, save and invest your money, it shouldn't come as a shock that many people simply do nothing about retirement planning.

There are three ways to retire:

1. The bank way
2. The Wall Street way
3. The insurance way

Notice that none actually involves jumping into a fire. But, as an average investor, how are you supposed to know? You've got three choices and a slew of other choices within each choice. What do you do?

"Investing for retirement is extremely important and extremely confusing. It's not really surprising that investors are in a kind of limbo, paralyzed," said prominent behavioral finance expert Meir Statman on *Retirement Matters,* my weekly radio interview show.

Dr. Statman is the Glenn Klimek Professor of Finance at the Leavey School of Business, Santa Clara University, and author of "What Investors Really Want: Know What

Drives Investment Behavior and Make Smarter Financial Decisions." He literally wrote the book on recognizing and overcoming behaviors that get in the way of making sound financial decisions.

"Perhaps the best cure for investment decision paralysis is working with a financial advisor whose values align with your own," Dr. Statman recommends. "It's all about hiring a person who aligns their goals with your goals, someone who'll guide you through the seemingly endless investment options and help you make smart decisions based on your particular financial goals."[6]

THE IMPORTANCE OF FINDING THE RIGHT GUIDE

My family and I recently went on a whitewater rafting trip in the Smoky Mountains. It was our first adventure on the rapids, so we decided to hire a guide to assist us in the raft. As we began to glide through the gentle waters I noticed that my youngest son was losing interest fast. My middle son was listening diligently to the guide, and my daughter longed for rougher waters. I began thinking to myself, "Why do we even need this guy?"

About as fast as that thought went through my head, it felt like we fell off a cliff and into Class 4 rapids! My youngest son was bouncing around like a piece of popcorn, and it became immediately evident who the most important person in the raft was: our guide. He knows what types of mistakes a novice or average person makes, and he happened to know the rough waters of this particular river like the back of his hand. (After all, he had already been down it five times that day!)

The number one objective I had when we hit those rapids was to get my family safely back to land, and that was the guide's top priority, too. Our goals became perfectly aligned

Did you know...

Working with a "fiduciary" means working with a "registered investment advisor" as opposed to a "broker-dealer representative."[7]

as we successfully maneuvered down the river with each other's help.

Do you think whitewater rafting is really that different from retirement planning or choosing the right investments?

In the investment world the guide would be a "fiduciary." Financial advisors who are considered fiduciaries are required by law to put their clients' best interests first, before their own. It's their fiduciary duty to provide the very best solutions they can find for their clients.

Unfortunately, most financial professionals are not fiduciaries. Rather, they are only held to what's called a "suitability" standard, meaning that they need only find a product or recommendation that's deemed "suitable" for you. That doesn't necessarily mean it's the best option available, and it certainly doesn't mean it's the best option for *you*.

Let me be clear: Just because a stockbroker or other "money manager" isn't a fiduciary, doesn't necessarily mean they're out to bilk you out of your life savings. There's a big difference between being a con artist or swindler like Bernie Madoff, and a broker who's recommending that you invest in something that happens to benefit him as well. Having said that, however, there's arguably an even bigger difference between that stockbroker and the fiduciary who is bound by a very high standard of law to put the client's interests first.

Do yourself a favor and find a financial advisor who is a fiduciary – someone who's looking at your overall situation and not pushing products, but developing a strategy that's custom-fit to your particular situation and goals. In other words, someone you can trust if you hit the financial rapids.

CHAPTER 3

TOO MANY CHOICES, NO ROOM FOR MISTAKES

Pick the right advisor first and your
options come later.

Ginnie Maes, G-bonds, T-bills, CDs, IRAs, SMAs, SEPs, ETFs, fixed annuities, insured deposits, commodities, currencies, managed portfolios, munis, mutual funds, money markets... *Make it stop!*

How can anyone make any sense of all this? That is, anyone except the professionals who do it for a living. And, if you're looking for such a person, how do you choose the right one from among all the different people out there giving financial advice? Bankers, brokers, CFPs, CPAs, RFCs, IARs, RIAs, registered reps, insurance-only producers, financial consultants, and on and on.

Finally, assuming you do find an advisor, how do you know if you're actually being "advised," rather than simply being sold a financial product (or products)?

Yes, it can be mind-boggling, but here's a tip: Knowing the type of strategies that work for most retirees will help you define your path. You'll still have to answer some of the questions above, but the basic education you'll need to succeed lies within the pages that follow.

First and foremost, begin tapering off your mid- to high-risk investments as you get closer to retirement. Even if you've had some success "playing the market" in the past, investing for the future is a completely different animal. The older you get, the less time you have to recoup any kind of market losses or downturns. You want your money where it's protected, because you're going to need it to supplement your income during your retirement years.

Sounds simple enough, right? OK, so what exactly are mid- to high-risk investments? Conversely, which are low-risk and protected from market fluctuations? That's where it gets more complicated.

Time to break it down, which we've done in this diagram:

The Pyramid of Investing

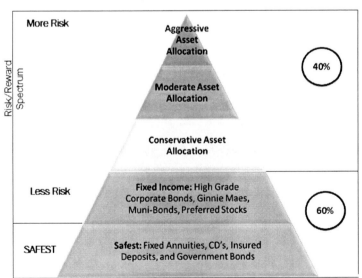

In the "Pyramid of Investing," we first split various investments into safer and riskier categories. There are four investment classes you should consider the safest: fixed annuities, CDs, insured deposits and government bonds. As long as you follow the guidelines for these products/investments you cannot and will not lose your principal.

As you move up the pyramid, the risk associated with various investment classes increases. Investments classified as "fixed income" carry the least risk, whereas portfolios that have an "aggressive allocation" carry the most risk.

Here's where you can factor in your own situation. As a general rule, you can start by using the "rule of 110" (modified to 100 for simplicity) to find your place on the pyramid. As an example, let's use a 60-year-old retiree. As a good base, a 60-year-old should put about 60% (give or take 10% more or less) of his retirement assets in products/investments positioned in the bottom two tiers of the pyramid (as shown in the chart on the previous page).

The rest of his money (30% to 50%) would be positioned in the top three tiers. How the money is allocated depends on risk tolerance, income needs in retirement and several other factors.

While it is not enough just to use this rule to position your assets, it does serve as a good measurement to see if you're "top-heavy" in your retirement risk. Everyone's situation is different, but this example emphasizes the importance of having safety associated with your investment strategy and portfolio. And, I should add, the importance of fully understanding the risks associated with each product/investment class.

Most workers enter retirement with almost all of their retirement dollars at risk, even though they think a majority of their money is protected. Why? In large part,

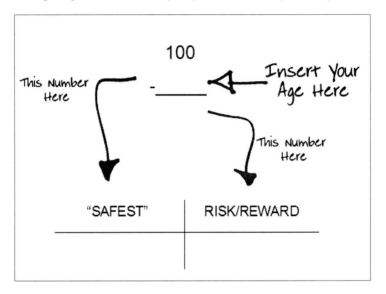

because Wall Street-oriented brokers and money managers characterize fixed income investments as "safe" to their clients. (Conservative, yes, but still subject to the ups and downs of the stock and bond markets.)

Dealing with this type of "advisor" – I use the term loosely here – is like playing a word association game. You say "safe," and they hear "conservative." Or, worse yet, you say "safe," and they think, "no commission, no can do." Ever wonder why the Wall Street advisor keeps telling you to "hang in there, it'll come back?" (Yet another reason why you should be working with a fee-only, fiduciary advisor, but more on that later.)

You rarely see advertisements for no-risk investment vehicles like government bonds, fixed annuities, CDs or insured deposits. Why? Perhaps it's because those vehicles are not a pivotal part of a Wall Street-oriented advisor's arsenal. That means that they (Wall Street) can't charge a fee on the protected products/investments you see in the bottom tier of the pyramid. But, for the retired or close-to-retired investor, these vehicles offer some distinct benefits:

- No loss of principal (if the terms and guidelines of those products and investments are followed)
- 5% to 8% accumulation for income only
- Protection and peace of mind for your financial future

Don't underestimate the value of that last one! Just ask the scores of people who over-invested in mutual funds and other investments characterized as "low risk" and now are left wondering what happened to their nest eggs.

Did you know...

Three-month CD rates in the 1980s topped 20%, while three-month CD rates in August 2011 averaged 0.263%.[8]

Here's an intriguing fact: Ten years ago, the CDs that investors "locked themselves into" at 5% outperformed the stock market. (And those investors didn't have to obsessively check their account balances or the market closing prices to see if they were making or losing money.) **Let me reiterate: Investing for retirement income is different than investing for growth.** We're going to talk about this more in the next chapter, but I'll give you three easy tips for starters:

- Never believe anyone who says you can average 10% a year on money that is at risk, because they "have the formula."
- Always preserve at least part of your money in products that are protected from market volatility – the base of the Pyramid of Investing, if you will.
- Get someone good in your corner – a retirement income specialist who understands your specific situation, knows the ropes, and is personally invested in helping you achieve your financial goals:
  - Someone who is a fiduciary
  - Someone who will build a plan for you, not take one off the shelf
  - Someone who helps you understand all of your options
  - Someone whose top concern is protecting and preserving your money

Throughout my career in the financial industry I have encountered hundreds and hundreds of people seeking investment advice, and I have yet to meet someone who told me they wanted to lose money. Every single one wants their money to grow. And many people have been burned by greed – promising and hoping, only to come up empty.

That's where the retirement income specialist comes in:

- To completely understand each individual or couple's specific financial situation
- To ground clients' expectations in reality, not greed
- To develop just the right investment solution to meet each client's needs
- To develop reliable and guaranteed income[9]

It's not necessarily easy, but it's definitely possible – and nothing beats seeing retirees you've helped lead a comfortable lifestyle in their later years.

Think of your retirement portfolio in the same way you would about planting a sapling fruit tree. When the tree grows and gets bigger, it matures and produces fruit every year. All you have to do is keep the tree alive. Retirement income planning is not really so different. When you retire (mature) you want your money (tree) to produce income (the fruit) that you cannot outlive (the tree dying).

How do you keep the tree from dying?

CHAPTER 4

WILL YOUR RETIREMENT MONEY "GO THE DISTANCE"?

Our lives are lasting longer, but is our money?
Don't get fleeced by taking the wrong advice!

Extreme stock-market swings, low investment returns, lower interest rates and plummeting real estate values have destroyed the finances of many people who want to retire and those who already have. Sadly, the majority of these people could have protected their hard-earned assets had they only switched their investment track earlier from "accumulation" to "preservation."

What does that mean, exactly?

There are three distinct phases in your financial life: accumulation, preservation and distribution. Understanding these phases as well as how and when to move from one to another is absolutely critical to your long-term financial well-being and success.

PHASE 1: ACCUMULATION (SAVING)

This phase lasts from the time a person starts working (usually in their 20s) until they retire (whenever that may be). During the accumulation phase the investor is building up savings with the intention of having an adequate amount

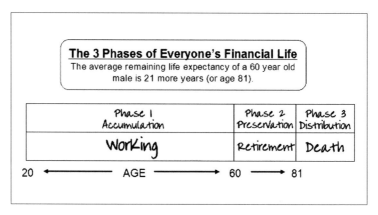

of money for retirement. In deferring spending in favor of investing, individuals are growing their savings over time. In general, the longer the accumulation phase, the better their chances of meeting financial goals for retirement.

Brokers and money managers are typically specialists for investors in the accumulation phase of their financial lives. An accumulation specialist focuses on allocating money into growth investments. Almost 100% of the time, virtually all of the invested assets are subject to risk during this stage.

Investors at this stage in life have a time "cushion" to recoup losses and deal with the ups and downs of the market. That cushion shrinks, however, as you move closer to retirement. It's at this critical juncture that an investor's focus must shift from asset accumulation to asset preservation.

Think about it. If you're planning to retire, say, in two years, that doesn't leave much time to make up for any market losses. Your nest egg will soon be your livelihood, and your investment approach must be realigned to keep it protected.

PHASE 2: PRESERVATION
(INCOME AND RETIREMENT)

As a person approaches retirement age there's a shift in importance from the continued accumulation of savings to the preservation and (for most) the spending of those accumulated savings. Preventing the erosion of principal and making plans for distribution become the priorities.

Most people make a huge mistake when moving from the accumulation phase into the preservation stage. After

Did you know...

89% of 77 million+ baby boomers are not strongly convinced they will live comfortably in retirement.[10]

years of investing in risk-type funds (often aggressively), it can be very difficult to taper off the risk and make the transition to a conservative mindset. Failing to do so has produced a very real problem the majority of Americans face today: the fear of running out of money before they die.

Working with a preservation and distribution specialist when nearing or entering retirement should be the first move you make. In order to successfully develop a portfolio that will reduce your risk and provide an income plan you cannot outlive, you must find someone who is willing to take some money "out of the market." (Brokers and Wall

Street-type advisors make their commissions on money "in the market," so it will be tough to find one who'll recommend making a change. Ever heard the saying, "Hang in there..."?)

PHASE 3: DISTRIBUTION (DEATH)

In the distribution phase, your assets and "legacy" are passed on to your beneficiaries and loved ones. Anything you leave behind will then change ownership according to your last wishes.

While it seems easy to construct a will to divvy up your assets, it is, in fact, much more complicated than most people imagine. Things like estate taxation ("death taxes")

Did you know...

According to the TransAmerica Center for Retirement Studies, the single greatest concern in retirement today is the fear of running out of money.[11]

and probate can throw a wrench right in the middle of things. All too often, family members and loved ones are forced to deal with a long, drawn-out legal battle with probate court and/or estate attorneys to settle everything.

Would you rather your loved ones have sufficient time to grieve and get back on track with their lives, or to get caught up in a legal fiasco that can significantly reduce the monetary value of your estate?

We are preservation and distribution specialists, not accumulation specialists. Working with a preservation specialist who has a relationship with a distribution specialist is key.

Rather than simply worrying about where to invest your money, your advisor should be determining the best path to protecting your money from loss while minimizing unnecessary taxation and providing the most reliable income possible. By positioning your assets accordingly and developing a bulletproof estate plan, your family can avoid probate altogether.

NEW GOALS, NEW MINDSET, NEW STRATEGIES

For 20, 30 or 40 years you've been in the accumulation phase, saving and trying like crazy to make your savings grow. You've worked hard, you've made sacrifices. As we discussed in the last chapter, you may have put some money in riskier investments, which you could do because you had time on your side – time for the market to adjust in your favor, or even time to rebuild lost principal.

Now you're entering, or have entered, the preservation phase. What changes? For starters, you don't have a regular paycheck coming in. You might have Social Security and/or pension income, which is great, but it probably doesn't match what you brought in before.

At this point what you have saved becomes absolutely critical. You don't have time for risk or room for lost principal due to stock market volatility. The chart at right hammers that point home.

In the chart I have illustrated the rate of return that's required to get back to even given each specific percentage lost in a given portfolio.

The middle column illustrates the rate of return you need if you are not withdrawing any money from your investments for income. The right column illustrates the rate of return you need if you are taking 5% of your portfolio out each year for income purposes.

Do you think this is alarming? This chart doesn't even factor in inflation or the fees you're paying that are coming out of your account balance!

Your savings are your bread and butter now. If you lose a loaf, you'll need two to replace it, and where will the money for the extra one come from? Not Social Security or your pension; you're living on that. Not your savings; that has to last the rest of your life.

You need guaranteed income. No risk, no chances, no unexpected fees or legal wrangling. By changing the way you invest your money, you can lead a more comfortable and secure retirement.

Have you ever lost sleep at night because you're worried about your investments losing money? Are you wondering whether or not you'll have any money left 10, 20, even 30 years from now?

IF YOU HAVE LOST....	Without taking money out for income... % NEEDED TO RECOVER TO EVEN	While taking a 5% withdrawal for income.. % NEEDED TO RECOVER TO EVEN
5%	5.26%	11.11%
10%	11.11%	17.65%
15%	17.65%	25.00%
20%	25.00%	33.33%
25%	33.33%	42.86%
30%	42.86%	53.85%
35%	53.85%	66.67%
40%	66.67%	81.82%
45%	81.82%	100.00%
50%	100.00%	122.22%
55%	122.22%	150.00%
60%	150.00%	185.71%
65%	185.71%	233.33%
70%	233.33%	300.00%
75%	300.00%	400.00%
80%	400.00%	566.67%
85%	566.67%	900.00%
90%	900.00%	1900.00%
95%	1900.00%	NEVER
100%	NEVER	NEVER

Quite frankly, you might need a new financial advisor. Even if the one you've been working with all these years has been terrific in helping you build your savings, that's probably what they're best at, not retirement income planning and protecting your assets. No criticism intended – helping people accumulate wealth is certainly honorable work, and many people are great at it.

But that isn't what you need anymore. You need someone who knows retirement income planning inside and out, someone who can help you protect your money in a safe place so you can finance your lifestyle through the remaining years of your life.

Better yet, you need an advisor who can show you the right amount of money you should be protecting in retirement. Here's the bottom line: As you can see on the chart below, the average person's life expectancy in this day and age has gone up dramatically.

Planning for a retirement income you couldn't outlive was much easier to do 20 years ago. Back then most employees

Life Expectancy at Birth, by Race and Sex, 1950 to 2004 [12]

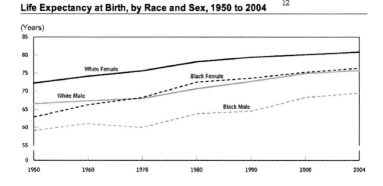

had a pension to fall back on. Social Security was relied on to supplement pension benefits, not as a primary source of income. For most, these two checks were more than enough to get by on.

FAST FORWARD TO THE PRESENT

As we discussed in Chapter 1, the traditional "three-legged stool" is wobbly at best. Pensions have given way to defined contribution plans – primarily 401(k)s – which were never meant to replace traditional pensions. When 401(k) plans came about, they were meant for extra tax-deferred savings to augment a person's overall nest egg, not to be the overall nest egg!

And so the problem facing our nation was born. More than 10,000 baby boomers (most of them without a pension) will enter retirement every day for the next 19 years. They are now forced to take their accumulated savings from their years of hard work and create a pension on their own – and most people's chances of doing so successfully aren't very good.

Despite all that, I have some good news for you. In the coming chapters I will show you what you need to do to overcome these obstacles.

CHAPTER 5

SURVIVAL OF THE FITTEST

*Retire with confidence, not with
your fingers crossed!*

W e've already talked about the importance of "knowing yourself" – as in, understanding the parts of your personality and background that can sway your financial judgment. Aside from preventing your own missteps, there are several other challenges we need to "knock out" before we win the bout.

There are 10 major obstacles you will likely face that could cause you to diverge from the track of retirement financial success. In Chapter 2 we covered the first: your own behavioral tendencies. But even if you can develop a strategy for removing emotion from your investing, there is still a long way to go. Let's talk about the other nine hurdles you need to clear to financially survive in retirement.

GREED

Unfortunately for you, plain old greed can get in the way of making smart, informed decisions about your retirement finances. When most investors make money on Wall Street they immediately start trying to time the market, which is one of the hardest things to do in investing. Like a gambler in a casino, most people just don't know when to walk away, or to sell an investment.

When gamblers are ahead at a blackjack table they'll usually begin to bet larger amounts because they're playing with the house's money. More times than not, the larger bets lead to larger losses, and faster than you can say "double down," they're in the hole. But that's not the end of it. Rather than walking away from the table, the new sensation of, "I need to win back at least what I started with," takes over.

You know what happens next. Before you know it you've lost all of your chips and are left wondering why you even sat down at the table to begin with. Investing in the stock market is no different. Most people who gamble really can't afford to lose money, and a lot of people who play the market can't afford to, either.

NO WRITTEN PLAN

I can't tell you how many times I've met with retirees or pre-retirees who tell me that they have a plan for their retirement. Then, when I ask them about the plan, they give me an asset allocation chart showing how their broker invested their money.

If you are one of these people, someone who believes that their "pie" (an asset allocation between different stocks, bonds or mutual funds) is a written financial plan, let me apologize in advance for breaking the news to you: **You do not have a written financial plan!**

Ask yourself a few questions about your current path:

- When I need to start taking income from my "plan," what strategy do I have in place to do so?
- How does my investment plan decrease the amount of fees I pay each year?
- If the market cycles again (as it will continue to do as long as Wall Street exists), what steps should I take to protect the money I need to produce income for my basic living expenses?
- The last time I sat down with my financial advisor, did he or she tell me how this plan should eliminate my fear of running out of money and protect my income for the rest of my life?

An honest-to-goodness investment plan answers these questions, and more.

A CLOSED MIND

Knowing that something is wrong with your portfolio or your investment style is only half the battle. The problem many have is actually convincing themselves that they need to make a change. Rejecting any suggestions for adjusting your investment strategy or refusing to look at alternative ways to invest can have devastating effects on your retirement.

Think of it in this way. If you are moving from the accumulation phase of your financial life into the preservation stage, you are entering unfamiliar territory. For the past 20 to 40 years

Did you know...

Half of U.S. workers who are at least 45 years old have never tried to calculate how much money they will need to live comfortably in retirement.[13]

you've invested fairly consistently in riskier stuff, knowing you have time to deal with the twists and turns the market will throw your way. Entering retirement is a mandate for you to move in a different direction. It's human nature to be uncomfortable with change. But you now have less time to recoup losses, less money coming in from wages, and you have to develop a plan to make your money last as long as you do.

Open your mind to change, or your money could wither away a lot faster than you can afford.

RETIRING TOO SOON

Beware of targeting a specific retirement age without reviewing your budget and developing your retirement number (more on that at the end of the list). Making it to retirement is the ultimate ending of a storied career. However, your accumulated savings, your income needs and your targeted retirement date may not add up.

The last thing you want to do is decide to retire without knowing if it's feasible. A lot of folks have come into my office telling me they are ready to retire, and when we go through the numbers, we find that they simply can't afford to yet.

The days of retiring at the milestone numbers of 62, 65, 68 or 70 are over. Retirement is largely dependent on whether or not you have the funds to do so.

SPENDING TOO MUCH

Spending too much in retirement can cause you to run out of money way too soon, plain and simple. When I sit down with someone to help them develop their retirement number (again, more on this at the end of the list), I make them

Did you know...

About 33% of investors don't know
how they are paying for the investment
advice they receive, and another 31%
think their broker or advisor provides
investment advice for free![14]

consider a variety of factors before they decide how much money they need to get by during retirement.

A good starting point is to determine how much you need to cover your basic core living expenses, plus what I call your "joy" expenses – the little extras you enjoy now, such as the occasional fancy dinner, nice birthday gifts for your grandkids, and so on. (More on joy expenses later in the chapter.) Together, these are the bare minimum costs to support your lifestyle.

If you can afford to factor in other expenses, such as a vacation home or travel, then you should. However, factoring these expenses in when the numbers show you could run out of money as a result makes absolutely no sense. It's time to know your budget!

PAYING TOO MUCH IN TAXES

I know taxes burn a lot of people. I can only imagine what taxes might be in the coming years and decades as our government tries to make up our ballooning national debt. Yet, to a certain extent, you can control what you are paying at the end of the year. A lot of times simply shifting your accounts into tax-deferred or tax-sheltered vehicles will help. In other cases your dividends could be costing you more than you want to pay.

An investment plan that positions your dollars in vehicles that are tax free or highly tax efficient will go a long way toward reducing excess taxes. Unfortunately, many advisors are not particularly concerned about the impact of your investments on your tax amount owed. Do you think your accountant is reducing your taxes? Think again! Most accountants simply "account" for your money. They really have no skin in the game that would push them to try to lower your taxes.

So the responsibility often falls on your financial advisor; however, it's simply not a priority for most. During your last meeting with your "advice-giver," what was the response when you asked what strategy is in place to reduce your tax bill?

PAYING TOO MUCH IN FEES AND COMMISSIONS

No matter where you put your "risk" money on Wall Street, you will pay a fee. Fees on risk money are unavoidable, and if you're not careful, they'll add up to a lot more that you'd imagine.

I have found that the majority of investors have absolutely no idea how much money they are paying annually in fees. If you think you do, I challenge you to tell me. In fact, I'm betting that you don't even know where to find them. Have you read your variable annuity or mutual fund prospectus? There's a reason they're written by attorneys!

Reducing your annual investment fee total can be done easily by reducing your risk. If you're working with a fiduciary, he or she is required to directly disclose any fees to you. However, as we discussed in Chapter 2, the majority of financial professionals aren't fiduciaries; they are only held to a "suitability" standard, which doesn't require them to fully disclose the fees before you invest.

LOSING MONEY SAFELY

Congratulations to those of you who have put money in safer accounts (like CDs or government bonds) for your retirement. I applaud you for taking the initiative to protect some of the money you'll need to live on for the rest of your life.

Having said that, for those of you who invested in those CDs and government bonds during the "great recession" years and the economic time immediately following it, you might want to reconsider the investment vehicles you're using. In an earlier chapter we outlined that three-month CD rates in December of 2010 averaged 0.95%. We call this "losing money safely."

Your principal is protected; there is no doubt about that. However, by overinvesting in low-interest, low-yield vehicles, and factoring in an assumed inflation rate of 3% (a conservative estimate), your purchasing power would decline by 2.05%.

NOT KNOWING "YOUR NUMBER"

This can be the most significant obstacle to attaining your retirement goals. Yet clearing this hurdle – if done correctly – can eliminate many of the first nine barriers we discussed.

Have you ever seen the TV commercial for a financial company that shows retirees carrying around large numbers? There's a man walking around with a big number (like $1,453,675) under his arm. The number represents the final net worth he needs to achieve before he will be able to retire with financial security. In the commercial, the people find great satisfaction in knowing that the day they hit that number, they will be able to retire worry-free.

What a misleading commercial! You need to calculate your number before you even begin writing your financial plan or figuring out whether or not you're retiring too soon or spending too much money.

This is very important:

Your number *isn't* the total net worth you need to amass before you retire. It's the amount of money you plan on spending each month during retirement.

How much money are you spending each month?

Retirement Income Goal:	$5,000.00
Social Security Benefit:	($2,100.00)
Pension Benefit:	($1,000.00)
Other Income:	($350.00)
Retirement Income SHORTFALL:	$1,550.00

You need to fund this number with your accumulated retirement assets!

ASCERTAINING YOUR NUMBER

Referring to the example above, **the top line – the retirement income goal – is "the number."** In this case, it's $5,000. To do your own calculations, leave that line blank for now, and move on to the income lines.

You might already know your monthly **Social Security** income. If so, fill it in. Same with your monthly **pension** benefit. If you don't know those amounts, check out the Social Security statement you get each year. It should tell you how much money you'll get each month if you retire when you're 62 years old, when you reach full retirement age (usually 65), or when you're 70. If you are or will be getting a pension, do the same (in most cases the pension plan provides similar information about how much you'll receive at various retirement ages).

The **"other income"** line is for things like part-time job wages, or a business you run out of your home.

To ascertain your retirement income goal – the number you absolutely must have to finish the formula – you need to take much more into consideration:

- **Your day-to-day living expenses** – Your house payment, property taxes, utility bills, food and healthcare expenses, and so on.

- **The extras, your "joy" expenses** – This is where you slot in all those things you've been putting off for retirement. The cruise, restoring the old Harley, taking flying lessons, updating the kitchen, visiting the grandkids on the West Coast a couple of times a year, and so on. It's important to factor in both the extras you enjoy today as well as your retirement dreams. The last thing you want is to be forced into a significantly different lifestyle or to forego your longtime goals just because you didn't do a good job planning your finances.

On the next page is a budget worksheet outlining both your basic expenditures and your joy expenses. (You can also print out a copy from NoIncomeWorries.com.)

In this sample worksheet, the retirement income goal is $5,000 per month. When you complete the worksheet with

BUDGET WORKSHEET	
CATEGORY	MONTHLY AMOUNT
EXPENSES	
HOME:	
Mortgage or Rent	$0.00
Homeowners/Renters Insurance	$100.00
Property Taxes	$500.00
Home Repairs/Maintenance/HOA Dues	$50.00
Home Improvements	$50.00
UTLITIES:	
Electricity	$50.00
Water and Sewer	$20.00
Natural Gas or Oil	$70.00
Cell Phone Bill	$150.00
FOOD:	
Groceries	$400.00
Eating Out/Lunches/Snacks	$300.00
HEALTH & MEDICAL:	$400.00
Insurance (medical, dental, vision)	$200.00
Fitness	$30.00
TRANSPORTATION:	
Car payments	$0.00
Gasoline/Oil	$300.00
Auto Repairs/Maintenance/Fees	$50.00
Auto Insurance	$50.00
DEBT PAYMENTS:	
Credit Cards	$0.00
Other Loans	$0.00
ENTERTAINMENT/RECREATION:	
Cable / TV / Videos/Movies	$110.00
Computer Expense	$40.00
Hobbies *This includes your*	$100.00
Subscriptions and Dues *"Joy" Expenses*	$50.00
Vacations	$300.00
PETS:	
Food	$80.00
Grooming, Boarding, Vet	$50.00
INVESTMENTS AND SAVINGS CONTRIBUTIONS:	
401k or IRA	$0.00
Stocks/Bonds/Mutual Funds	$0.00
Savings	$500.00
MISCELLANEOUS:	
Clothing	$100.00
Toiletries, Household Products	$100.00
Gifts/Donations	$150.00
Grooming (Hair, Make-up, Other)	$200.00
Miscellaneous Expense	$500.00
TOTAL (RETIREMENT INCOME GOAL)	**$5,000.00**

your own information you'll know "your number" – your retirement income goal.

DEALING WITH THE SHORTFALL

If the income number is smaller than your number, you have a retirement income shortfall. (Most people do, by the way.) This is where your savings come in – to make up the difference. Developing an investment strategy to accomplish this involves three basic steps:

- **Project your number of retirement years** – Now that you know your number, you need to estimate how long you'll need to sustain that steady stream of monthly income. When calculating this, please don't underestimate how old you'll live to be. Even if the average life expectancy is 78 years old, figure you'll live to at least 90 or 95. Believe me, you don't want to put yourself in the position of outliving your money. Aim high.

  Say you're 55 years old now, and you want to retire when you're 65. Figure you're going to live to 100 (hey, your grandmother is still alive and well at 97!), so that would be 35 years of retirement for you.

- **Plan for inflation and future expenses** – Here's where a lot of people blow it! They carefully calculate their income number and estimate their retirement years, then neglect to factor in inflation and other expenses that may arise in the years to come (long-term care, for example, or other health-related services not covered by Medicare). Don't make the same mistake, or you might end up with less than you need to get by comfortably. We typically adjust the income target up 3% to 5% each year to ensure that the income you need will be there when you need it.

- **Work with an experienced retirement income professional.** After reviewing your situation, the specialist might advise you to delay retirement a few years so you can bolster up your savings. (That might not be welcome news at the time, but better to deal with it sooner rather than later!)

Regardless of when your retirement years begin, the guidance of a skilled retirement specialist is critical to ensure that your savings are in a protected place to produce the income you'll need to live comfortably throughout your later years.

Yes, with smart planning, that really is attainable. In the next two chapters we'll talk about the basic investment strategies to make it happen.

CHAPTER 6

WHY YOU NEED YOUR MONEY IN A SAFE PLACE

Because it's now about INCOME!

Here's a recap of what we've covered so far:

- **The traditional idea of retirement – living primarily off Social Security and pension payments – is no longer realistic.** Personal savings are essential to maintaining a comfortable standard of living after you retire.

- **We humans carry a lot emotional baggage that can get in the way of making sound financial decisions.** You've got to cut through that clutter to invest rationally, not emotionally.

- **Guaranteed income should be your top retirement priority.** The only way to achieve it is through products such as fixed annuities, CDs, insured deposits and government bonds – not investments with hope alone.[15]

- **The older you are, the fewer risks you should take with your money.** At this point the focus should be on safety and guaranteed income, not growth investing.

- **To formulate your plan, you've got to know "your number"** – how much money you'll need to support a comfortable lifestyle throughout your retirement years.

Now that you know your number, it's time to figure out how to protect the money that will support you during retirement – the money you're counting on to make up the shortfall between your total fixed living expenses and your Social Security income (and benefits from a pension, if you have one).

You will always have fixed living expenses, and the money needed to cover them should always be in a protected place. "The key is having safe income for your fixed expenses," said Alicia Munnell, a leading authority on retirement income policy.[16] Remember the Pyramid of Investing introduced on page 35? At the base of the pyramid were examples of the safest money places – fixed annuities, CDs, insured deposits, immediate annuities and government bonds.

Now take a look at the Pyramid of Investing vs. the Pyramid of Expenses, below.

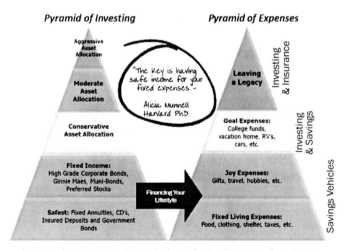

You should be using savings vehicles to fund at least your fixed living expenses. If you don't want to change your lifestyle in retirement, you should include your "joy" expenses as well.

Basically, you're dividing your assets into two general categories: protected accounts and risk accounts. The protected accounts will provide you with the income needed to finance your lifestyle in retirement. When you divide your assets like this, you'll separate your emotions from your investing. Why is this so important, you might ask? So you have income that is protected and guaranteed. With your emotions removed, you're less likely to make bad investment decisions and get caught in a downward market spiral. Instead, you can sit back and relax because your income is guaranteed – a regular retirement "paycheck" that isn't tied to the ups and downs of the economy or the stock market.[17]

Makes perfect sense, right? Let's look at a case example, below, that contrasts the "Wall Street" way of retirement income (risk and no guarantees) to my ILIP (Inflation Laddered Income Plan), which is guaranteed.

Bob and Mary Jones

- Both 65 years old

- They have $1,175,000 saved for their retirement

INCOME NEED:		
	Basic Living Expenses	$2,500
	Joy Living Expenses	+$2,500
	TOTAL Monthly NEED	$5,000
	Bob & Mary Social Security	<$2,000>
	Bob & Mary Pension	< $500>
	RETIREMENT INCOME SHORTFALL	$2,500

First we must understand the difference between income and returns. When we retire, remember, we are going from the accumulation phase of our financial life to the preservation and distribution phases. We will now need to take income from our money to make up our shortfall. When we were accumulating our assets and had varied returns over time, say 10 years, our average return would have been the same no matter what order in which the returns occurred.

As you can see in Charts 1 and 2 (below), the order of your returns really doesn't matter when you are not making annual or monthly withdrawals from your accounts. The sequencing of returns in both examples ends up being an

Chart 1   Unfavorable Return Sequence

Year	Beginning Year Balance	Annual Return	Annual Withdrawal	Year End Balance
1	$100,000.00	-25.00%	0	$75,000.00
2	$75,000.00	-15.00%	0	$63,750.00
3	$63,750.00	10.00%	0	$70,125.00
4	$70,125.00	12.00%	0	$78,540.00
5	$78,540.00	12.00%	0	$87,965.00
6	$87,965.00	14.00%	0	$100,280.00
7	$100,280.00	14.00%	0	$114,319.00
8	$114,319.00	15.00%	0	$131,467.00
9	$131,467.00	18.00%	0	$155,131.00
10	$155,131.00	25.00%	0	$193,914.00

8.00% Average Return

Chart 2   Favorable Return Sequence

Year	Beginning Year Balance	Annual Return	Annual Withdrawal	Year End Balance
1	$100,000.00	25.00%	0	$125,000.00
2	$125,000.00	18.00%	0	$147,500.00
3	$147,500.00	15.00%	0	$169,625.00
4	$169,625.00	14.00%	0	$193,373.00
5	$193,373.00	14.00%	0	$220,445.00
6	$220,445.00	12.00%	0	$246,898.00
7	$246,898.00	12.00%	0	$276,526.00
8	$276,526.00	10.00%	0	$304,178.00
9	$304,178.00	-15.00%	0	$258,552.00
10	$258,552.00	-25.00%	0	$193,914.00

8.00% Average Return

average 8% return over a 10-year period. No matter when the losses or gains take place in the example, you still end up with $193,914 after 10 years.

In Charts 3 and 4 (the "Wall Street way"), the owner of the account needs income of $7,000. Now the order of returns has a major effect on the account balance. The examples below depict the same scenario as in Charts 1 and 2, but we are now withdrawing money to supplement retirement.

Chart 3   Unfavorable Return Sequence

Year	Beginning Year Balance	Annual Return	Annual Withdrawal	Year End Balance
1	$100,000.00	-25.00%	$7,000.00	$68,000.00
2	$68,000.00	-15.00%	$7,000.00	$50,800.00
3	$50,800.00	10.00%	$7,000.00	$48,880.00
4	$48,880.00	12.00%	$7,000.00	$47,746.00
5	$47,746.00	12.00%	$7,000.00	$46,475.00
6	$46,475.00	14.00%	$7,000.00	$45,982.00
7	$45,982.00	14.00%	$7,000.00	$45,419.00
8	$45,419.00	15.00%	$7,000.00	$45,232.00
9	$45,232.00	18.00%	$7,000.00	$46,374.00
10	$46,374.00	25.00%	$7,000.00	$50,967.00

8.00% Average Return

Chart 4   Favorable Return Sequence

Year	Beginning Year Balance	Annual Return	Annual Withdrawal	Year End Balance
1	$100,000.00	25.00%	$7,000.00	$118,000.00
2	$118,000.00	18.00%	$7,000.00	$132,240.00
3	$132,240.00	15.00%	$7,000.00	$145,076.00
4	$145,076.00	14.00%	$7,000.00	$158,387.00
5	$158,387.00	14.00%	$7,000.00	$173,561.00
6	$173,561.00	12.00%	$7,000.00	$187,388.00
7	$187,388.00	12.00%	$7,000.00	$202,875.00
8	$202,875.00	10.00%	$7,000.00	$216,162.00
9	$216,162.00	-15.00%	$7,000.00	$176,738.00
10	$176,738.00	-25.00%	$7,000.00	$125,553.00

8.00% Average Return

Remember, the title of this chapter is "Why you need your money in a safe place." These charts show exactly what can happen if you fail to protect your principal from market losses.

Notice in Chart 3 that in the first year the account loses 25%, and then 15% the next year. But remember, now we are withdrawing money on top of those losses, so the account needs an even greater return just to get back to even. For the remainder of the 10-year period, the stock market rebounds and the account owner sees a number of solid overall returns. Wait a minute, the account averages 8%, and it's only worth $50,967? This is why you must protect the money!

In Chart 4, the first eight years of returns are rather amazing. However, the last two years of returns take a bite out of the account value. Once again, in both examples, the average rate of return over the 10-year period is 8%. Yet in Chart 4 we end up with $125,553, and in Chart 3 we end up with $50,967. The order of returns matters.

The moral of the story is that you have zero control as to where the stock market will be (up or down, in a recession or during a prospering economy) when you decide to retire or take income.

- Do you want to subject your retirement income to market gains or losses?
- Do you want income that's guaranteed or variable?
- In our example, is the individual living off the 8% average return from the portfolio or the income of $7,000 a year?

- Are you comfortable taking the chance of running out of money, or do you want a guarantee that you'll always have income to live on?

- Do you want to be in control of your financial destiny when you retire?

Using the "Wall Street" method of retirement, you simply have to hope that you receive consistent returns throughout the course of your retirement, because you are making annual withdrawals from your nest egg. The $7,000 income is the most important part, not the return! The average return was 8%, but a few bad years would severely increase your chances of running out of money. **The bottom line: Forget about the returns and DON'T CHANGE YOUR RETIRE-MENT INCOME!**

Which is why you should have an ILIP (Inflation Laddered Income Plan). Now let's get back to Bob and Mary from page 65. Instead of using the "Wall Street" method of retirement, they could simply separate their assets into the two categories we mentioned before: safest accounts and risk accounts.

USING ILIP (INFLATION LADDERED INCOME PLAN)

If Bob and Mary were to separate the money that produces the income they need in retirement from the money they would like to see grow, they wouldn't have to worry about stock market returns or running out of money and their income stopping. The money that they need for income should be positioned in the safest category, and whatever is left over can then be positioned at risk (if they choose).

Let's break it down a bit further. If Bob and Mary were to position approximately $525,000 using an ILIP from their $1,175,000 nest egg into safer products, they could meet their $2,500 a month income shortfall while guaranteeing that they never run out of income. They would achieve financial peace of mind because they wouldn't be subjecting their income to risk or stock market losses, and they could take risk freely on the money they have left (approximately $650,000).

This method of retirement provides a solid base that covers their lifestyle, while giving them growth potential in the event they want to leave a legacy to their heirs, buy something, or simply adjust their income down the road.

Yet very few people actually do this. Why? We are so used to focusing on rates of return that we lose sight of our real goal: reliable income. Retirement is about cash flow, not about returns. To develop reliable income, you should position your dollars in products that can deliver it.

For the balance of this chapter I will prove to you that you can achieve guaranteed income and investment growth while maintaining peace of mind during retirement.

WHY ILIP?

Rather than hoping for returns and the right timing, you should be setting up an income plan that is guaranteed. You can't do it with money that's at risk. It must, at all costs, be done with safe money.

The ILIP strategy I use is one of the steps in our Financial GPS (Guided Planning System), which we'll talk more about in subsequent chapters.

Depending on your time frame, your financial situation, and a multitude of other factors, most people have enough money accumulated by the time they reach retirement to create an ILIP.

With an ILIP you have a series of guaranteed income payments that would start now or at a desired point in the future. The income payments are guaranteed (backed by a legal reserve insurance company) to come in each and every month, and they are set up to last your entire lifetime.

I'm not talking about sinking your money in to a "safe" account that is paying 1% and drawing it down to nothing. I'm talking about using some of the best annuity products in the industry to produce a reliable income stream that you will never have to worry about. (At the time this book was published, cash flows ranged on average from 5% to 7%, depending on the account holder's age.)

The best thing about the plan is that it factors inflation into the payments at multiple points in the future. Depending on your time frame, your financial situation, and a multitude of other factors, most people have enough money accumulated by the time they reach retirement to create an ILIP.

There's one problem, though: You can't do it on your own. To set it up properly you need to work with an income planning and distribution specialist. Your broker or money manager won't do it. Your accountant won't do it. Why? Because they will tell you to put it in the market so you can make more money. They will tell you that you need higher returns. Most will simply just sell you product rather than develop a plan for your income. Most don't even understand the principle of distribution to begin with.

Don't we all want to produce guaranteed income in retirement? Isn't that what we work our entire lives to achieve? I told you at the beginning of the book that pensions have virtually disappeared, and the facts point to success in retirement for those who still have them. Shouldn't the retirees who were not blessed with lifetime pensions be creating their own if they can?

If you are still reading this book, my guess is that you are someone who would sleep a whole lot better at night if you had a guaranteed paycheck or pension. If that's true, just keep reading. I will show you what you need to do.

Let's build an Inflation Laddered Income Plan.

CHAPTER 7

INFLATION-ADJUSTED INCOME FOR LIFE

Set the strategy now so you don't have to change your lifestyle during your retirement years.

L et's get into the nitty-gritty of building and preserving your lifetime income, the second phase of your financial life. As we discussed in Chapter 4, the main goals in this phase are to provide guaranteed income and prevent the erosion of principal.

But wait a minute... How can you do both at the same time? If you're taking money out of a retirement asset account to make up for an income shortfall, doesn't that reduce the principal? And what about the 4% withdrawal rule you hear about? Can't you just take 4% of your money per year and never run out of money? That's what Wall Street suggests.

Developing an income plan that you can rely on in retirement takes strategic planning that includes some of the safest and most reliable income products/investments, making periodic adjustments to your income due to inflation, and enlisting a plan to do so that doesn't ever run out of income as long as you live.

We talked about dividing your assets into two categories in the last chapter. Your safest money should be used to develop an income plan in retirement. But how much money do you need to put there? How do you develop a plan that will produce a retirement paycheck equal to your income shortfall without reducing your principal drastically or drawing your money down to nothing? As we discussed in the last chapter, I have developed a strategy called ILIP (Inflation Laddered Income Plan). By using an ILIP you can develop laddered, lifetime income that uses the safest and most reliable income products/investments to produce a retirement paycheck that eliminates your income shortfall. When the plan is set up correctly your income will go up with inflation over time.

Inflation plays a pivotal role in developing lifetime income. It is one thing to develop a paycheck that is guaranteed for your lifetime, but if the paycheck ends up being too small in 10 years because of future inflation, you might end up having to go back to work, or worse yet, change your lifestyle to adjust to your new budget. To develop a bulletproof income plan, you need to understand how inflation could affect your money while you are in retirement.

INFLATION: THE CRABGRASS IN YOUR FINANCES

Most people go about planning for inflation the wrong way. We all know what inflation means. A dollar today might not be worth a dollar in the future. Somewhere down the road, the price for goods and services will go up due to inflation. You have experienced this yourself.

Did you know...

Since 1982, our country has experienced
95% inflation (based on a Consumer
Price Index of 195).[18]

In the 1950s bread cost around 14 cents a loaf. Today you're lucky to find one for under $3. Gasoline? The price for a gallon of gas was around 20 cents in the 1950s. In the last few years gas prices have averaged about $3 per gallon.[19] In 1958 a brand-new Corvette cost about $4,000. Today a stock Corvette with basic features starts at $50,000 retail.[20]

No matter where you live, inflation will affect the price of the goods and services you purchase, and it will affect your retirement if you let it. Most investors know this, and they believe they are factoring in future inflation properly. It never seems to fail. When I ask someone what plan they have in place to hedge against future inflation, everyone gives me the same answer: higher returns.

The average investor is focused on higher returns on their entire sum of money so they don't have to worry if inflation comes into play. What if you lose money on that portfolio?

Wall Street will try to convince you that you can achieve a 10% average return on your money. Have you ever averaged 10%? In my career, out of thousands and thousands of people, I can count on one hand those who have actually averaged 10% returns.

The Standard & Poor's 500 Index averaged 9.14% growth per year for the 20-year period December 30, 1990 through December 30, 2010. Pretty close to 10%, right? Did you know that in that same time period, the average investor who had money in equities earned a market return of only 3.83%?

"Planning" for inflation this way is dangerous. Are you with me? **Inflation does not affect *all* the money you have accumulated; inflation only affects your income.** You don't need to subject your entire nest egg to risk. Inflation only affects the money you plan on spending during retirement. You do, however, need to factor inflation adjustments into that money.

USING AN ILIP (INFLATION LADDERED INCOME PLAN)

We know that "inflating" the money we spend (not all the money we have saved) is the right move. The hard part is determining how much to inflate that money, when to make the adjustments for inflation, and the vehicles or strategies you can use to do so.

With an ILIP you can use your retirement income shortfall (the number you need your retirement money to fund) to calculate a scheduled income payout that is guaranteed to come in as long as you or your spouse is alive. It also incorporates periodic inflation adjustments to that income and provides you with the flexibility to make additional income adjustments at any point in time.

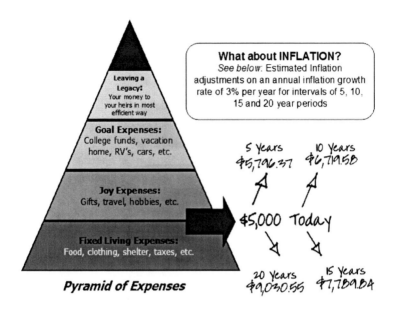

Pyramid of Expenses

From 1990 to 2010 the inflation rate was 2.57% per year.[21] As you can see on the next page, adjusting for this is extremely important.

Let's round the inflation rate up to 3% to be safe. At an inflation rate of 3% annually, a monthly income need of $5,000 today is a monthly need of $9,030.55 in 20 years.

Without planning for income adjustments you may be faced with changing your lifestyle. Do you really want to force yourself to choose between going out to eat every Friday night with your friends (the way you have been doing for the last 20 years) or paying the gas bill on time?

The key is to develop an Inflation Laddered Income Plan that will cover your retirement income shortfall.

Let's use the example of Bob and Mary Jones from page 65. They have a $5,000 a month income need in retirement.

However, because of their Social Security benefits and a small pension, they only need their assets to provide them $2,500 per month. So we need an ILIP that will provide Mr. and Mrs. Jones with the extra $2,500 they need to live comfortably in retirement.

THE ILIP (INFLATION LADDERED INCOME PLAN)[22]

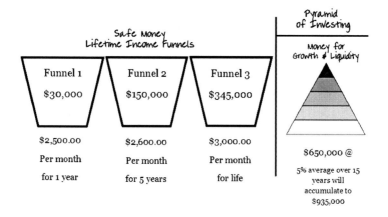

For the sake of our example, let's say that Mr. and Mrs. Jones' retirement income of $2,500 per month is to start immediately. Let me walk you through a step-by-step sample ILIP that would guarantee a lifetime $2,500 paycheck that is adjusted for inflation along the way.

In the ILIP plan above you can see how Mr. and Mrs. Jones divvy their $1,175,000 into $525,000 in the safest money accounts and $650,000 into the riskier accounts to grow over time.

The safe money in the funnels is used to fund a personal pension that is insured and guaranteed to last a lifetime.

Funnel 1 provides income of $2,500 per month for one year. In years two through six, Funnel 2 will provide income of $2,600 per month. Starting in year seven, Funnel 3 will produce income of $3,000 per month for life (no matter how long Bob and Mary live). This money will provide income to cover basic living expenses and joy expenses that Mr. and Mrs. Jones can rely on at all times throughout the remainder of their lives.

The $650,000 that the Joneses didn't put into their income plan is then positioned in whatever way they want to invest it. I advise most retirees to take lower amounts of risk on this portion of their portfolio, using fixed income investments, REITs, preferred stocks, bonds or other risk assets that produce dividends and high yields.

You may also use the money that is positioned at risk as a further hedge against inflation. In the Jones example, $3,000 may not be enough at some point if the pace of inflation remains steady throughout their retirement. If that winds up being the case, they can use money that's accumulating in their "growth and liquidity" section to produce supplemental income so that they can continue to enjoy their lifestyle.

Either way you spin it, the most important aspect of the ILIP is the income. On the next pages we'll break it down in more detail, funnel by funnel.

FUNNEL 1: IMMEDIATE INCOME

The first funnel of the ILIP will provide an immediate "paycheck" to make up for Mr. and Mrs. Jones' $2,500 per month shortfall.

Year 1

$30,000

Payments for

12 months:

$2,500.00/month

You want to use safer products here that are fully liquid and develop a systematic draw-down for a short period of time (preferably one to five years). The reason for this is that while this first income funnel is paying the money needed immediately, the other two funnels are building up principal that is lost due to payout.

In our example, if we put $30,000 into the first funnel and draw it out over a 12-month period, Bob and Mary will have the $2,500 a month that they need.

FUNNEL 2: FIRST INFLATION ADJUSTMENT

The second funnel of the ILIP will begin paying income in year two, when the first funnel is depleted.

This is also when our first inflation adjustment will occur.

Years 2-6

$150,000

Payments for

60 months:

$2,600.00/month

After one year at 3% inflation, we now need approximately $2,600 a month instead of $2,500. The second funnel will last five years.

If we position approximately $152,000 in this funnel, using the $525,000 that Bob and Mary have set aside, we will be able to provide guaranteed income payments of approximately $2,600 per month for a period of five years. During this time the final funnel of the ILIP will continue to defer payments and grow, recouping most of the principal that has been spent throughout the first six years of the income plan.

FUNNEL 3: SECOND INFLATION ADJUSTMENT/LIFETIME INCOME

We make another inflation adjustment in the third and final income account in this version of the ILIP. (There are a number of custom versions of this plan that install more than three funnels or only two funnels.) Any future inflation adjust-

Lifetime Income

$345,000

Payments for life:

$3,000.00/month

ments will come from your growth money. This account will now be your base, guaranteed income for life.

After six full years of payments, Bob and Mary's $2,500 monthly income need has inflated to approximately $3,000 a month (or $36,000 a year instead of the $30,000 a year they started with). We want to set this funnel up so it will pay guaranteed income for the rest of their lives – income they will never outlive.

By positioning approximately $345,000 into this funnel, we can contractually guarantee a lifetime income payout of around $3,000 per month. The income will come in as long as Bob and/or Mary are living. When they die, their beneficiary(ies) will receive a lump sum of any balance that remains, or continue income payments moving forward.

The income benefit of a strategy like the ILIP is huge when you peel back the curtain and take a look at the numbers. In our example, if Bob and Mary were to die 20 years after they started their plan, they would have received a total of $690,000 in income from their protected income funnels! The money they stashed away for "growth and liquidity" would have grown to $1,173,972 if it averaged 5% over 20 years.

WHY DON'T MORE PEOPLE USE THIS STRATEGY?

I find it odd that some people avoid this method of planning because they are afraid to move away from the accumulation style of investing. Retirement is about enjoying the rest of your life. You shouldn't have to worry about what the stock market is doing and how it will affect your income. If you set up contractual guarantees using insurance or bank products that produce the exact amount of income you need at any point in time, you'll never have to worry about financing your lifestyle again.

Don't do it yourself. Work with a professional retirement specialist to guide you in selecting the right investment vehicles to meet the goals of your plan. As we discussed in Chapter 3, there are so many options out there, it just doesn't make sense for you to attempt it yourself. A specialist in this area can help you develop a plan similar to my ILIP. They should be aware of the best income-producing assets if they are a seasoned retirement income professional.

If you follow the steps I have outlined within the first seven chapters, you could be well on your way to a fantastic retirement built on guarantees, not hope. Even so, you haven't won the match yet!

The perfect income and investment plan is often destroyed due to a catastrophic illness or a medical spend-down of assets. In the remaining chapters I will outline the additional things you need to take into consideration if you want to make sure your retirement goes the distance.

CHAPTER 8

HOW THE PERFECT INCOME PLAN IS DESTROYED

More than half of Americans over 65 will need long-term care (LTC), which can wreak havoc with your guaranteed income plan. Build a wall between your health and wealth so you won't be caught cold if the need for LTC arises.

It's a subject none of us wants to think about, but ignoring it won't make it go away: At least 50% of those over age 65 will at some point need long-term care. The cost of nursing homes or assisted living facilities can easily reach $7,000 a month, and in-home services often cost even more. When this kind of help is necessary, the last thing you need to worry about is how to pay for it.

Many people mistakenly assume that Medicare covers these type of services. Wrong. **Medicare is health insurance, not long-term care insurance.** It may pay for part or all of medical care provided at a nursing home – skilled physical therapy for rehabilitation after surgery or an accident, for example. But it does not cover "custodial" care, the type of daily living assistance required by many elderly people.

Medicare does provide fairly reliable coverage for medically necessary, acute care issues. That said, it's important to know what it doesn't cover, including hospital stays or doctor visits beyond what the program allows, some prescription medication costs, and a number of other costly services and items that can add up very quickly.

Unlike Medicare, Medicaid can pay for nursing home care and even some in-home healthcare. **The problem with Medicaid, however, is that you have to be all-but-impoverished to qualify for it.** There are stringent eligibility rules about what assets you can have (or keep) to qualify for Medicaid benefits, requiring most middle- and upper-middle class seniors to "spend down," or divest, most of the assets they have worked a lifetime to build.

Where does that leave you? In most worst-case scenarios, either:

- Spending the majority of your savings to pay for in-home care or to live in a nursing home
- Spending down the majority of your assets to quality for Medicaid

Basically, you lose either way. Now don't read this and think to yourself, "Yes, but my husband (or wife, or children) will take care of me." While it might be true that a family member, or members, will be happy to help, you've got to consider the huge impact that full- or even part-time caregiving has on a person – particularly someone who's experiencing age- or health-related challenges of their own, or who's already stretched by other job, family and financial responsibilities.

Let's examine why this is such a huge problem.

ODDS AND COST

Let me give you some facts that may help you change your viewpoint on the matter. According to the 2011 Genworth Financial Cost of Care survey, 67% of people age 65 and older will need some sort of long-term care (LTC) in their lifetimes, whether they like it or not. There is a two in three chance that in your lifetime you will need long-term care.

For those of you who answered, "I will never need it," let me show you what kind of cost you could be looking at in the event that you end up a part of that 67%.

NATIONAL MEDIAN RATES FOR LTC SERVICES[23]		
SERVICE TYPE	HOURLY/DAILY/YEARLY	ANNUAL COST
Home Health Aide	$18.50 PER HOUR	$48,100.00
Adult Day Health Care	$60 PER DAY	$21,900.00
Assisted Living Facility	$3,261 PER MONTH	$39,132.00
Nursing Home (Semi-private room)	$193 PER DAY	$70,445.00
Nursing Home (Private room)	$213 PER DAY	$77,745.00

As you can see in the chart above, long-term care in almost any capacity is extremely expensive. Without some sort of insurance to help you pay for it, you could end up broke. Whether you spend down your remaining assets to pay the bill, or simply to get to Medicaid eligibility, you will end up forfeiting any chance of passing on money to your loved ones or heirs. **Remember, odds mean nothing when it happens to you!**

Fortunately, you can create a barrier between your health and wealth, so if you need long-term care you'll have a plan in place to protect your money and your income. Most people think this is a decision about purchasing LTC insurance or not. However, most people aren't aware of all of the ways to pay for LTC. For most of this chapter I will talk about building this barrier to protect your assets, as well as the psychological tendencies that get in the way of making a prudent decision.

TWO MAJOR PSYCHOLOGICAL FACTORS

Let me describe a few reactions people have when it comes to making a decision about whether or not to protect themselves from the financial impact of long-term illness.

- **The "I will never need long-term care" people.** Have you ever heard the term "reflex response"? It can also be referred to as a "knee-jerk" reaction. According to Merriam-Webster's dictionary, a knee-jerk reaction is when someone responds to a situation in a readily predictable way.

   If you are one of the people who will instantly say, "I will never need long-term care," you are fooling yourself! Just curious...how do you know? This answer is a knee-jerk reaction to what should be a common part

---

Did you know...

In 2007, over $3.5 billion in long-term care insurance claims were paid out.[24]

of a complete financial plan – a problem that almost everyone will do anything to avoid talking about.

Why would someone give this answer? For the most part, it's because they simply do not want to plan for this part of their life. No one wants to actively plan for the day they have to enter a nursing home or assisted living facility, much less plan for how they will fund the cost.

We are accustomed to being independent adults, and moving into a nursing home or assisted living facility can be viewed by many as sacrificing that independence.

That said, a lot of people simply refuse to spend money on something they may never need (LTC insurance). More often than not, these folks truly think they will just fall over dead someday and never need care, so why would they spend money on LTC protection? Here are some common "reasons" I have heard over the years:

- "My grandfather died at 68 in his sleep."
- "My father died of a heart attack."
- "My mother had a stroke and died 30 days later."
- "No one in my family ever needed care before."
- "My parents and grandparents all died in their 70s and never needed care."
- "I'll end my life rather than go into a nursing home."

For the most part, these people recognize the need, but refuse to believe they might ever need care. They think of the premiums they will have to pay as "lost" money.

For example, Mr. Jones paid $3,500 into his LTC policy for 20 years, totaling $70,000. He then died quickly and never needed the policy. So the $70,000 of premiums he paid into the policy were for nothing.

You can see why some people would be a little apprehensive about making this kind of an investment. Yet this kind of thinking is like saying, "Darn! For the last 20 years I've paid for homeowner's insurance, and my house never burned down!"

Had Mr. Jones had the right kind of benefit on his LTC policy, all premiums paid would be returned to a named beneficiary. More on that in a minute.

- **The "My children or spouse will take care of me if I need long-term care" people.** OK, I get it. You understand that you'll probably need LTC at some point. The statistics say you have a two in three chance of needing it in some capacity, so you've thrown in the towel and agreed with me that you may need care in the future.

  So you think your children or spouse will take care of you if you need long-term care? Let me ask you a question: Have you run that by them? Your spouse, maybe, but your kids?

  If you are in this group, then you know what I am talking about. You realize that you may have a need for assistance, but refuse to plan for professional care because you believe your family members and/or other loved ones will be there to help in your time of need.

  This could be true in some cases. I know there are an abundance of people around the world who have this arrangement. I urge you to exercise caution about this, though. Ask yourself a few of these questions:

□ Do I really want to place this burden on my spouse or children?
□ What if my spouse also needs care?
□ Are my spouse or children in the right financial situation to provide care?
□ What kind of financial burden will this put on my children if they are not ready for this? (Will they still be working? Will they have kids in college?)
□ Will this method actually save me or my family any money?

Often times people believe that by avoiding a nursing care facility or assisted care they will save money. However, medical expenses and the cost of care – even when provided at home by a family member – can, and will, take its toll on your assets.

Consider your spouse providing care first. You have to realize that he or she may not always be in the best position to be your primary caregiver. Sure, it would be nice if you could stay at home and continue living the way you are used to living, but let's be practical.

If your spouse develops the need for care, your situation takes an immediate 180-degree turn. You both need care that will soon become too expensive for your retirement budget.

Ultimately, you'll end up depleting your accumulated assets, and when you pass away, your spouse will be left in a very precarious position. Compound that by the very real possibility that he or she will need care after you're gone, and the situation drastically worsens. When it comes to your kids providing the care, it's too easy to assume that they will be in the right financial position to do so.

Your children will probably be working and saving for their own retirement. They are really not at liberty to spend their qualified assets to assist in the cost of providing care. Plus, work schedules and other family responsibilities will demand most of your kids' time. You must consider other options.

OPTION 1: LONG-TERM CARE INSURANCE

A lot of people think they have to fit an LTC insurance premium into their monthly budgets. Most people would never own this type of insurance if they had to do this.

I'll be the first to admit that LTC insurance premiums can be a huge expense. Trust me though, the alternative of doing nothing is much more expensive.

How do you pay for it?

Let's go back to Bob and Mary Jones. Take a look at the example on the next page.

Below is Bob and Mary's portfolio. They have positioned their assets into two categories. Let's say they get approved for an asset protection barrier of $162,000. This will provide a pool of money of $162,000 that Bob and Mary can spend before they ever have to touch any of their invested money.

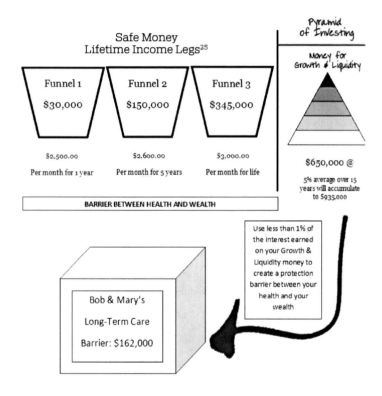

Rather than adding the LTC premium to their monthly budget, they can use a little bit of their interest each and every year to pay the premiums, as shown in the example.

OPTION 2: ASSET-BASED LONG-TERM CARE INSURANCE

Asset-based long-term care insurance is an enhanced type of life insurance with an LTC insurance option attached to it. It works like a savings policy with a feature you can switch on in the event that you need to pay for LTC. Rather than losing the benefit base you have paid in over the years, the unused amount will be paid out to your beneficiaries. Check out the example below.[26]

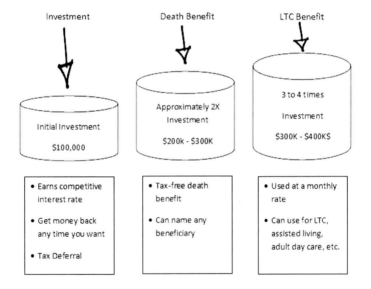

Investment	Death Benefit	LTC Benefit
Initial Investment $100,000	Approximately 2X Investment $200k - $300K	3 to 4 times Investment $300K - $400K$
• Earns competitive interest rate	• Tax-free death benefit	• Used at a monthly rate
• Get money back any time you want	• Can name any beneficiary	• Can use for LTC, assisted living, adult day care, etc.
• Tax Deferral		

Most LTC insurance salesman will never tell you about this option. Why? The companies they work for want them to sell LTC insurance.

The problem with this type of planning is that you literally have to take at least $100,000 of your retirement dollars off the table to designate it solely for LTC. This works best for people who have accumulated a decent amount of assets.

Whether you opt for traditional LTC insurance or asset-based LTC insurance, the important thing is that you are comfortable with your plan and how you will pay for it.

OPTION 3: DO NOTHING

This strategy says that you will pay for your care dollar for dollar with your accumulated assets. This may work just fine for some people.

If you choose this option, however, make sure that you know which assets you will use to pay for the care. Also consider the taxability of that money.

Individuals who have accumulated at least $1 million for retirement – and are not using that money to produce supplemental income – are good candidates for this option.

The people who have saved $200,000 to $600,000 in assets are the most vulnerable when it comes to this strategy. Remember, results vary widely depending on how much money you are spending from your accumulated retirement savings. I always recommend that you have a written plan if you are going to self-fund this risk.

When it comes right down to it, I suggest you have a qualified estate attorney help you protect your assets from the Medicaid spend-down process. It's no secret that the Medicaid system is broken. Since the DRA (Deficit Reduction

Did you know...

According to the American
Association for Long-Term Care
Insurance, the average need (or stay)
of care is 904 days.[27]

Act) of 2006 was passed, qualification for the program has become increasingly difficult, virtually stripping retirees of their hard-earned assets.

With the right legal team it may be possible to "impoverish you on paper," thereby sparing you from the draconian Medicaid spend-down process. Fair warning, though: It's much more difficult to do today than in the past.

Net-net, if you have enough assets, funding LTC costs out of pocket could be a viable option. In some cases we're able to build this option into an ILIP that guarantees your income to double for a certain period of time to offset the additional cost of care that is needed.

But before you go pushing LTC insurance planning out the window, think about the potential cost to you and your loved ones of doing nothing.

P hew! Throughout these last eight chapters we have explored the complex world of retirement investing, primarily for income. You have the general blueprint in your hands to develop a sound income plan and a written investment plan, as well as protection from a catastrophic illness.

Before you ride off into the "retirement sunset," I want to remind you about one last thing. What happens if you don't spend all of your money before you die? Although for many that possibility is growing more and more unlikely, there are retirees out there who pass away and want to leave the remainder of their assets and money to their spouses, children, grandchildren, friends, churches, schools and charity – instead of government, taxes and attorneys.

That's what we'll cover in the next chapter.

CHAPTER 9

PLANNING FOR THE END

What happens to your money after you're down for the count? Decide now and get your estate documents in order. Then forget about it and enjoy life!

Planning for what happens to your assets after you die doesn't have to be a morbid business. Like any other aspect of financial planning, you need to know the facts, understand your options and work with a trained professional to help you translate your individual needs and priorities into a workable strategy.

Estate planning begins with several basic documents that an experienced estate attorney can help you prepare and, if desired, amend from time to time. A good financial team should have a person like this who helps their clients in accordance with the financial plan that has been developed.

One of the most important factors in developing total financial security is making sure your professional team (your financial advisor, your estate attorney, and even your accountant) are on the same page for your benefit.

In my firm, I have a partnered estate attorney who I rely on to assist my clients with setting up an estate and succession plan that will help them avoid probate and paying too much in tax, while passing their legacy on to their beneficiaries in the best way possible. I'm now going to turn this chapter over to her, and she will show you the most important items to focus on when thinking about your estate plan.

Let me introduce Margie T. Karl, our partner in helping people properly plan for distribution, the final phase of their financial life.

Following are Margie's insights and recommendations.

Often times people think that drafting a simple will is all they need to do in the area of estate planning. After all, as long as you lay out who should get what, it shouldn't be much more complicated than that, right? It's your stuff, it's your money. Why should anything else matter?

As it turns out, estate planning is much more complex. Death is something that most people rarely want to talk about. Nevertheless, there are a number of death-related questions you should consider on behalf of your loved ones.

- How can you minimize the tax consequences for your heirs?
- How can you avoid probate and the effect it could have on your loved ones in their time of grief?
- Should you set up a trust?
- Are your accounts and your estate set up properly so your loved ones don't have to go through a legal fiasco when you pass away?

Throughout this chapter I'll explain some of the basics of estate planning. We'll start with the foundation documents and move on from there.

FINANCIAL POWER OF ATTORNEY (POA)

A properly drafted, signed and notarized financial or general durable POA allows someone you appoint (your "agent") to make financial decisions on your behalf when you're alive but unable to manage your affairs. In this document you spell out exactly what duties the agent can perform, so work with an experienced estate planning attorney who can help you fully understand your options and directives.

Have you ever heard of the "powerless power of attorney?" In laymen's terms, this means that the power of attorney your estate planner drafted doesn't have any teeth behind it.

The document must be written properly to grant your appointee the ability to manage your assets. If you are deemed incapacitated in terms of making decisions regarding your own health or your finances, and your POA is ineffective, you will find yourself in trouble.

Did you know...

Without an appointed power of attorney, the interested party must begin legal proceedings to become legal guardian, which could cost thousands of dollars in out-of-pocket expense.[28]

LIVING WILL

A living will is a legal document that allows you to express your wishes to medical professionals in case you become incapacitated. In a living will, you can outline whether or not you want your life to be artificially prolonged in the event of a devastating illness or injury.

A living will is often combined with a "healthcare proxy," which allows you to designate someone to make healthcare decisions for you if you become incapacitated. The living will and the healthcare proxy together make up what's called an "advanced healthcare directive."

LAST WILL AND TESTAMENT

A will is a legal document that lets you tell the world who should receive which of your assets after your death. It also allows you to name guardians for any dependent children. Without a will, the courts decide what happens to your assets and who is responsible for your kids.

Wills do have limitations. In particular, the beneficiary designations on financial accounts, insurance policies and other assets take precedence over wills, so it's important to make sure your beneficiary designations are up to date and reflect your wishes.

For example, say you list your husband as the primary beneficiary on your retirement plan at work, but then you get divorced and marry someone else. If your first husband is listed as the account beneficiary, he will receive those assets at your death – even if your will says otherwise.

A will also allows you to name your executor, the person who will be in charge of your estate. Before you select an executor, make sure you understand the tasks he or she will need to perform, which include distributing your property, filing tax returns and processing claims from creditors. Your executor should be someone you trust completely – don't forget to ask if he or she is willing to take on such a big responsibility.

Dying without a will, or dying "intestate," means you have no say over who receives your assets, and your estate must go through probate. This leaves your heirs and the court system the complex and costly job of wrangling over who should get what.

HOW DOES PROBATE WORK?

Quite simply, probate is ugly. When you die, your heirs must go to probate court and petition the court to "be allowed" to use your assets. The heirs must report to the court the assets that have come in, the assets that have gone out, and to whom they are distributed.

Probate court can become quite expensive due to the length and detail of the process. Not only will your heirs or beneficiaries incur the court costs involved with going through probate court, but in most cases they will also require the assistance of a lawyer to help see them through. So attorney costs come into play as well.

Did you know...

At death, any creditors involved in the life of the deceased are notified of the death, in which case they have a certain time frame to report said debt to the estate.[29]

One of the primary reasons people leave money to their loved ones is to help pay the bills that laying themselves to rest will incur. If your heirs are faced with probate court, they will not have immediate access to the funds or assets that you leave behind. So the onus is now on your loved ones to pay for your funeral expenses before they have access to your funds. Until petition is made in probate court, they will also be responsible for paying your debts to creditors after you've passed on.

Even after petition is made in probate court, the process tends to drag out longer than anyone expects. In fact, the average time in probate court is well over a year! Can you imagine looking down on your loved ones as they are forced to deal with your funeral expenses and your debts to creditors, all the while going through a year or more of probate court?

The best way to deal with probate is to avoid it altogether!

TRUSTS

A trust is a legal entity that lets you put conditions on how certain assets are distributed upon your death. Trusts also can help minimize gift and estate taxes. A properly written and funded trust can save time, money, and headaches for your loved ones as they deal with your death. Your trustee can access funds to pay for funeral expenses and/or debts that you leave, then distribute the assets in accordance with your last will and testament.

There are many different kinds of trusts, each applying to specific situations. An experienced attorney can help you establish one that fits your needs.

A **revocable living trust** is one of the most common trust types, as it is used as an alternative to a will. This trust will pass assets on to your loved ones while avoiding probate. With a revocable living trust, you appoint a successor trustee, which is similar to an executor of a will. While you are living, you are in charge of your trust. When you pass away, your named successor then takes over as the trustee. This individual is in charge of the assets in your trust or your estate.

Here is where the difference between a trust and a will becomes important. Unlike a will, when you have a trust and you pass away, your assets transfer into the trust ("funding" the trust). Because the trust is a "living" legal document that continues to "live" after you pass, your assets that are funded into the trust are fully accessible by the trustee.

Did you know...

Wills must be filed in probate court to be executed, which means they become public documents.[30]

This begs the question: Do you need a trust or do you need a will?

Sometimes it is enough to have a will. For example, if the will owner's assets fall under the current tax-exempted amounts on the state and federal inheritance tax and are properly titled for their beneficiaries, a will should suffice.

An **irrevocable living trust** is generally established to reduce taxes and/or deal with specific portions of the estate. The main difference between a revocable and irrevocable living trust is that the latter cannot be changed and the assets inside cannot be accessed during your lifetime. Following are a couple of examples of irrevocable living trusts:

- **Spendthrift trust.** If you're worried about your beneficiaries spending all your assets "in one place," you might want to consider this type of trust. The spendthrift trust is designed to deliver benefits to beneficiaries on an as-needed basis. Rather than providing instant access to all of the funds, you can prolong the benefit you leave while protecting the money from creditors.

- **Charitable remainder trust.** As you might have guessed, the charitable remainder trust is designed for people who want to leave a sum of money to charity. It also works well for people who want to reduce their taxes. You get a nice write-off when the donation is made, and there are strategies that can be used to purchase a life insurance policy with the tax savings in the event you want to leave a chunk of cash to your beneficiaries.

The advantage of having both a financial planner and an attorney on the same page for your benefit is priceless. I am very excited to be part of the four-step review process that the author of this book, Bill Smith, and his team have created. The final step of their financial Guided Planning System (GPS) is the estate review, which allows individuals to link their financial strategy with a sound estate plan that protects and passes their assets on in the most efficient and effective way.

Now back to you, Bill.

Now that you understand the basic estate documents as well as the difference between owning a trust and a will, it's important to know that you can draft these documents to extend their normal benefits. For example, you might be able to deliver more of a tax benefit or more of a financial benefit to your beneficiaries.

Proper legacy planning involves the drafting and use of your estate and financial documents in tandem, which also means that your financial planner and estate attorney must work together for the plan to work properly.

Before we wrap up this chapter, I want to talk about an often-overlooked strategy that can be very effective for some people. It's inexpensive and can leave a legacy for your heirs without requiring a change your retirement lifestyle.

THE LEGACY IRA

When this strategy is set up properly it can save your beneficiaries on taxes as well as restrict the amount they – as well as creditors – can access in the event your loved ones were to get sued.

Essentially, a legacy IRA "stretches" your IRA money that remains at your death over your children's and grandchildren's lifetimes. By restricting the distribution of the asset to the RMD (required minimum distribution), your heirs only get a portion of the money as a distribution each and every year for the rest of their lives. Taxes are extremely reduced, because the only portion of the money that is taxable to them is the amount received annually, rather than the entire distribution.

If you use the proper accounts, the money will continue to grow and stretch over the life expectancies of your named beneficiaries. The benefit that is paid out to your heirs using this strategy can greatly exceed the value of your IRA when you die. How? Growth on the account monies not distributed through RMDs continues to grow, tax-deferred, as well.

With the right moves, you can even pass the money on **tax-free** to your beneficiaries through an "Insured Spousal Roth Conversion" or a "wealth replacement trust." (If you're working with an advisor who understands this type of planning, of course.)

For example, we can reposition a 65-year-old couple's $500,00 IRA so it passes on to their beneficiaries. The dollars will be stretched over the life expectancies of their children and their grandchildren, totaling in excess of $1.5 million.

Total distributions over the lives of the couple, their children and grandchildren will exceed $2 million. Now that's a legacy.

By the way, the bigger the IRA, the bigger the legacy.

CHAPTER 10

HIRING THE RIGHT ADVISOR FOR YOU!

*How to find a professional whose
goals are aligned with yours*

This is where the rubber meets the road. Getting the right type of advice will make all the difference in your financial plan. Will you choose to protect your retirement and your income, or will you roll the dice?

I cannot stress enough the importance of the topics I have raised throughout this book. I hope that you take the knowledge you have garnered and put it to good use in making smarter decisions with your hard-earned money!

Even though I hate to say it, I know exactly what will happen for some of you. After you're done reading the book, you'll put it on the bookshelf or pass it on to someone else to read, and ultimately end up doing absolutely nothing about your own situation. That's right, nothing. It's human nature. We simply do not like change. Even if we can clearly see the benefits, even if the benefits are screaming out at us! For whatever reason, we'll still procrastinate.

Do you believe that knowledge is power? You do, right? Well, that's only partially true. It's the *application* of knowledge that's powerful.

Now I want to challenge you. I challenge you to take the answers to the questions you had and to do something about it. That is what this final chapter is all about. I know you can fix your problems – I have given you the training and the ammo you need!

The first step down this path is up to you. You need to find a team of financial professionals that will help guide you through the rocky terrain of retirement income planning. Here's the kicker: This team needs to be a team of "specialists," not "generalists."

Think of it this way: Would you go to a neurologist if your knee was hurting? An orthodontist if you had an earache? The same idea applies to your financial challenges. Most people continue to go to the same advisor and expect a different result. In other words, are you expecting your tried and true accumulation advisor to lead you through the preservation and distribution phases of your financial life?

Following are seven steps to find a team of financial professionals to assist you in developing a plan that works for you. By following these steps you will find a specialist that fits your needs. Read through them. They could save your financial life!

DON'T GO IT ALONE

You need to find a team of professionals who specialize in retirement planning and retirement income. The team should include, at a minimum, a qualified estate attorney, registered investment advisor, licensed insurance producer and an accountant. These professionals should share a like mindset with each other and you.

You might be thinking, "Why can't I do all the things you talked about in this book myself?

While some people do succeed in planning their retirement future on their own, several things tend to get in the way. Emotional attachment to their own money, for example, or not having the proper licenses to access certain products or investments.

The ones who truly win the "retirement game" are the folks who seek out assistance from a team of professionals who specialize in preservation and distribution planning. Then you develop a winning strategy, with the team's help, that encompasses all of your retirement goals and objectives.

IF IT SOUNDS TOO GOOD TO BE TRUE, IT PROBABLY IS

Watch out for financial "salesmen." A lot of them – including brokers and bankers – like to pose as a "financial advisors." Unfortunately, rather than advising you on what you should be doing with your money to meet your goals, they are simply selling you a product. There is a fine line you can draw in the sand that will help you determine if you could be falling victim to this. Use the questions on the next page to figure it out:

Did you know...

According to the Federal Trade Commission, more than half of all U.S. consumer injury reported comes from investment fraud.[31]

- **Is the advisor a fiduciary?** As we discussed in previous chapters, some advisors are merely held to a "suitability" standard, which means they need only find you a product that is suitable for your situation. Being a fiduciary means that by law, the advisor must find the best product available for your needs, and your needs must come before their own.

- **Did the advisor ask the right questions?** Did the advisor spend time with you asking important questions about what you want your money to do for you? Questions are important. Simply reading the answers to a risk questionnaire is not a reliable way to recommend an investment product. Your advisor should know exactly what your goals and objectives are for every investment piece of your retirement portfolio puzzle. Most importantly, your expectations of the investment should be in line with the advice.

- **Does the advisor team up with the right specialists?** One quick way to determine if you are dealing with financial "salesmen" is to take a hard look at their teams. Who do they work with, or do they work by themselves? Do they have employees? Do they only work with securities? Do they only work with insurance products? Do they work with a qualified estate attorney?

- **Are they pushing me to make a decision faster then I want to?** The tell-tale sign that financial advisors are nothing but salesmen is if they try to sell you a product vs. a plan. An advisor should take the time that is necessary to get to know you, ask you the proper questions, go over all of your problems and concerns with you, then draft a plan of attack to address your goals and objectives. The last part is how to fund it.

  Funding your plan is merely a process of reallocating your money to new investments that better suit your situation. There are a lot of great financial products available to you that you might not already know about, but most great products come with "strings attached." Make sure you fully understand what you are being offered and the strings attached to each.

WATCH OUT FOR COMMISSION BROKERS

How is your advisor getting paid? And for the amount that you are paying, do you think that you have received enough value? In other words, is the fee you are paying worth the advice you are getting?

> ### *Did you know...*
>
> According to the **Wall Street Journal** and **Morningstar**, there are expenses related to the buying and selling of securities that make a (mutual) fund two to three times as costly as advertised.[32]

Commission brokers make money on the transactions you make on your accounts. Buying. Selling. Holding money in the market. They want to make sure you have activity and remain in the market.

You must understand the key components of how your advisor is being compensated. Making sure your advisor is a fiduciary is a good place to start. Remember, no matter where you park your money in the "risk" world, there will be a fee associated with doing so. You can lower your fees by understanding all the investment options that are available to you.

If you choose to have money in the market and you want to lower your fees on that money, you must understand what you are paying now. The "Investment Fee Discovery" step in our Financial GPS (Guided Planning System) can show you that amount. (Visit NoIncomeWorries.com for more information.)

BEWARE OF ONLINE "RESOURCES"

Be careful about doing research online. It has become increasingly common to find the answers for anything these days by typing your question into Google. That does not mean, however, that the answer you find is the right answer. Just now, I typed the phrase "income planning" into Google, and 392 million results came up! That's information overload, and it can be a huge problem.

If you are going to do research online, you should be spending time researching a team of professionals to help you. Focus your efforts on finding someone who can meet your needs, someone who specializes in retirement income, preservation of assets, and estate planning.

DEMAND PROOF

Often times financial "salespeople" are very swift talkers. They may sound like the real deal, but are they? You need to demand proof. Ask the following questions. Their answers should give you some insight as to whether or not you are working with a true expert.

- **Have you ever been published in an industry periodical?** Industry publications look for real experts because they want their readers to get credible information. You need someone who knows their stuff.
- **Are you an author on your subject?** Even though there are financial professionals who are not authors but

are still credible sources, professionals who take time to write about their trade are clearly passionate about what they do. It's not easy to write a book, trust me! But the professional who is proud of the service they provide often has a published book to back it up.

- **Do you invest in your professional knowledge?** This is a good gauge of how current your advisor is on the economy, tax code changes, new laws and cutting-edge ideas and planning strategies.

  Our world is ever-changing. If advisors aren't investing in their own education, odds are that they're bringing old ideas and strategies to the table.

- **Do other professionals trust you to help their clients?** I am not talking about simple references here. When other professionals (estate attorneys, accountants, insurance specialists, etc.) refer their clients, it means they trust the advisor to do the right thing for their clients. That's a big endorsement.

BE SMART AND TRUST YOUR FEELINGS

Sometimes the best thing you can do is trust your gut. I always tell people, liking your advisor's services is one thing; liking your advisor is completely different. You should not only be happy with the service and performance your advisor provides, but you should like him/her, too.

I don't know about you, but it's hard for me to take advice from anyone that I don't really like. Your retirement advisor should be the last advisor you have, so it's important that you see eye to eye and get along well.

FIND AN ADVISOR WITH A "PROCESS"

One of my last pieces of advice is that when you narrow your list of advisors down to a few, take a hard look at each of their processes.

What kind of process do they take you through before they provide recommendations? Every financial professional is a little different. Even though it's possible that they will arrive at the same destination, it's highly unlikely they will lead you down the same road to get there.

Your main focus should be on working with someone who will lead you though a process, not sell you a product. Work with someone who will give you the solutions to your problems first.

I never recommend a product or investment type until I take someone through my process. Quite frankly, without doing so, I simply don't know enough about their wants, needs, and their overall situation to make a sound recommendation.

My process is called the Financial GPS (Guided Planning System). It's a proprietary planning process that guides you through a very thorough analysis of your current retirement portfolio. When people go through the GPS they walk away knowing more about their current financial position than they ever have before, and it allows us to become educated about their situation and what is most important to that person.

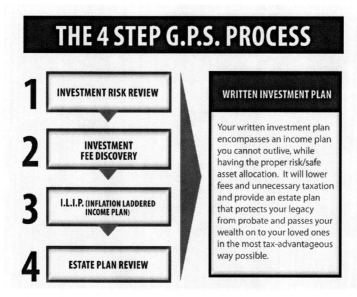

THE 4 STEP G.P.S. PROCESS

1 INVESTMENT RISK REVIEW

2 INVESTMENT FEE DISCOVERY

3 I.L.I.P. (INFLATION LADDERED INCOME PLAN)

4 ESTATE PLAN REVIEW

WRITTEN INVESTMENT PLAN

Your written investment plan encompasses an income plan you cannot outlive, while having the proper risk/safe asset allocation. It will lower fees and unnecessary taxation and provide an estate plan that protects your legacy from probate and passes your wealth on to your loved ones in the most tax-advantageous way possible.

I use four simple steps that you can see above. By taking someone through the process, I uncover their problems and potential problems, discover what they are paying in fees, show them how much risk they are taking, develop the framework for a custom ILIP (Inflation Laddered Income Plan) and, finally, give them a proper estate plan review with our recommended estate attorney, Margie Karl.

If you find someone who is willing to walk you through a process instead of sell you something, it's likely that you're taking a step down the right path.

I wrote this book because it is my goal to empower you to make the very best decisions with your money. I wish you the very best in retirement. Be proactive and educate yourself – if you have finished this book, you have already started to do so.

Now what are you waiting for? Go forth and knock out your retirement income worries FOREVER!

For more information about the ideas and strategies presented in this book, or to learn about additional publications from this author, visit **NoIncomeWorries.com**.

ACKNOWLEDGEMENTS

The author wishes to thank the following people for their contributions to this book:

Jarrett **Lang** spent countless hours interpreting my scribbles. He was a contributing editor on this project and influential in the overall production of this book. Thanks for all of your hard work, Jarrett! Jarrett is an insurance advisor at W.A. Smith Financial Group and specializes in providing asset protection and insurance-related income strategies for retirement.

He also serves as the co-host of my weekly radio show, *Retirement Matters.* He's in charge of setting up interviews with national guests and the production of the show's content each and every week. He graduated from Ohio State University and currently holds his Ohio Health and Life Insurance licenses.

Brad **Buckingham** is a financial advisor at W.A. Smith Financial Group and assists me on a daily basis with developing customized financial plans for clients of the firm. Thank you, Brad, for your contribution to Chapter 8, "How the Perfect Income Plan is Destroyed."

Brad is a specialist in the protection of assets in the event of a long-term illness. He graduated from Ashland University and currently holds his Ohio Health and Life Insurance licenses as well as his Series 66 license.

Margie T. Karl is W.A. Smith Financial's recommended estate and elder law attorney. She assists clients in the development of custom estate plans that eliminate probate and unnecessary estate taxation while providing assistance in passing on assets in the most efficient and tax-advantageous way.

She graduated from Marietta College and the University of Akron School of Law.

Margie specializes in financial law and elder law and is an integral part of step four of our Financial GPS (Guided Planning System). Thank you, Margie, for your contribution to Chapter 9, "Planning for the End."

APPENDIX

Chapter 1

[1] www.snopes.com/politics/socialsecurity/changes.asp

[2] Financial Status of the Social Security and Medicare Programs, www.socialsecurity.gov (Actuarial Resources section)

[3] www.businessinsider.com/scary-facts-about-the-coming-pension-crisis-2010-8#for-all-states-unfunded-pension-liabilities-equal-up-to-32-trillion-13

Chapter 2

[4] dalbar.com/Portals/dalbar/cache/News/PressReleases/pressrelease040111.pdf

[5] Cornell Center of Behavioral Economics and Decision Research

[6] Quote from interview with Meir Statman on Retirement Matters Radio, May 1, 2011, www.RetirementMattersRadio.com

[7] "Why Smart People Make Big Money Mistakes and How to Correct Them: Lessons from the New Science of Behavioral Economics" (Simon & Schuster, 1999), by Gary Belsky and Thomas Gilovich

Chapter 3

[8] www.moneycafe.com/library/codi.htm

[9] Product guarantees are subject to the financial strength and claims-paying ability of the issuing company.

Chapter 4

[10] www.abcnews.go.com/US/wireStory?id=13297597

[11] www.transamericacenter.org/resources/TCRS12thAnnual%20WorkerNewRetirementFINAL05162011.pdf

[12] Congressional Budget Office using data from National Center for Health Statistics, Health, United States (Hyattsville, Md., 2007), Table 27

Chapter 5

[13] online.wsj.com/article/SB10001424053111904491704576571223765726228.html

[14] www.investmentnews.com/article/20110608/FREE/110609950

Chapter 6

[15] Product guarantees are subject to the financial strength and claims-paying ability of the issuing company.

[16] Quote from interview with Alicia Munnell on Retirement Matters Radio, September 19, 2010, www.RetirementMattersRadio.com

[17] Product guarantees are subject to the financial strength and claims-paying ability of the issuing company.

Chapter 7

[18] www.inflationdata.com/Inflation/Inflation_Rate/HistoricalInflation.aspx

[19] www.fiftiesweb.com/pop/prices-1950.htm

[20] www.auto.howstuffworks.com/1958-corvette.htm

[21] DALBAR Inc. 2011 QAIB (Quantitative Analysis of Investor Behavior), Research and Communications division March 2011

[22] The lifetime funnel example is based on current rate availability at time of authoring. Guaranteed income annuity rates were used at time of authoring and are subject to change. Exact results mirrored to this example are based on rate availability and cannot be guaranteed. Please consult with a retirement income specialist for current rate information.

Chapter 8

[23] Genworth 2011 Cost of Care Survey - www.genworth.com/content/etc/medialib/genworth_v2/pdf/ltc_cost_of_care.Par.14625.File.dat/2010_Cost_of_Care_Survey_Full_Report.pdf

[24] www.aaltci.org/long-term-care-insurance/learning-center/fast-facts.php

[25] Premium price and "shared care" pool rates are subject to change and are not guaranteed. Rates used in this example were obtained from John Hancock's hypothetical illustration software. Rates and pool illustration are based on the following set of variables: a 65-year-old male and 65-year-old female, both non-smokers; Ohio based; Select Rate obtained, with John Hancock's Custom Care II plan.

[26] The example is hypothetical and rates are not guaranteed. The example makes no claims to specific products or investments and is general in nature.

[27] www.aaltci.org/long-term-care-insurance/learning-center/fast-facts.php

Chapter 9

[28] www.uslegalforms.com/powerofattorney

[29] www.probate.laws.com

[30] www.msnbc.msn.com/id/31748440/ns/business-personal_finance/t/jackson-death-illustrates-will-vs-trust-issue/#.ToTPteyoqSo

Chapter 10

[31] www.ftc.gov/reports/Fraud/invest.shtm

[32] online.wsj.com/article/SB100014240527487033829045750596909054870722.html

CPSIA information can be obtained at www.ICGtesting.com
Printed in the USA
BVOW020008070912

299578BV00007B/24/P